EVEN BROOK TROUT GET THE BLUES

JOHN GIERACH

ILLUSTRATIONS BY GLENN WOLFF

SIMON & SCHUSTER

NEW YORK LONDON TORONTO SYDNEY SINGAPORE

SIMON & SCHUSTER
Rockefeller Center
1230 Avenue of the Americas
New York, NY 10020

First Simon & Schuster trade paperback edition 2003

SIMON & SCHUSTER and colophon are registered trademarks
of Simon & Schuster, Inc.

For information regarding special discounts for bulk purchases,
please contact Simon & Schuster Special Sales at
1-800-456-6798 or business@simonandschuster.com

Designed by Chris Welch
Manufactured in the United States of America

13 15 17 19 20 18 16 14 12

The Library of Congress has cataloged the hardcover edition as follows:
Gierach, John.
Even brook trout get the blues / John Gierach.
p. cm.
1. Fly fishing.   2. Fishing stories.   I. Title.
SH456.G56   1992
799.1'755—dc20   92-7555
ISBN 0-671-77921-4
0-671-77910-9 (Pbk)

CONTENTS

"Motivation, if it ever existed as an agent in human affairs, is completely shagged out now. What drives people is a lot woollier than motivation."

—MARTIN AMIS

"Not everything is known about fly fishermen. As the researchers say, further study is indicated."

—CHARLES WATERMAN

1

FARM PONDS

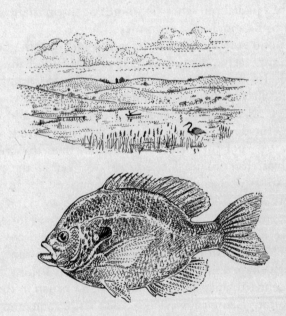

I THINK THE FIRST FISH I ever caught was a bluegill from a pond on my uncle's farm in Indiana, but I can't be absolutely sure. You'd think that would be something you'd never forget—like any number of other firsts I could mention—but although that memory would be no more than about forty years old now, it has become obscured by subsequent fish, of which, I have to say, there have been quite a few.

I suppose my first fish could just as easily have been a little bullhead from the creek at home, but there's something about that pond I can't get out of my mind.

I remember it as small, so, given the propensity of things from childhood to loom larger than they really were, it must have been tiny—maybe a few acres at the most. There were cattails growing at the shallow end and the water near the dike was deep enough to swim in, though I never thought it was all that inviting. There were too many weeds and sticks that seemed to want to grab you, and there was this morbid curiosity I had about what else might be down there. I never did get to be much of a swimmer.

The pond stood out in the open not far from the house; a low, unimpressive disk of water you could see from a long way off. Its banks were grazed-over pasture trampled to mud, and there were no trees for shade. The water was clear, though. I can remember wading in the shallows and watching the crawdads skitter along the bottom in front of me. Usually I'd spot their trails of silt first, then the creatures themselves. Eventually I overcame my fear of the pincers enough to try and catch them by hand, at least the little ones that were around in the spring. It wasn't easy.

There wouldn't have been much in the way of natural structure in the pond. It was set in a shallow draw with a seasonal stream running through it, so the bottom would have been shaped like an elongated bowl. But I think I recall Uncle Leonard sinking some old tires and brush in there for fish habitat. Leonard was a serious fisherman and knew about those things. I don't think they referred to it as "structure" then. I think they just called it "old tires and slash." They didn't call it "habitat," either. They just said the fish liked it.

One thing I remember clearly is the electric fence you had to cross to get to the pond. Uncle Leonard—being an advocate of one-trial learning—let me go ahead and touch it so I'd know why I was being told *not* to touch it. Leonard once told me, "Dogs and kids aren't good with ideas, but they learn well from experience."

In the beginning at least, I fished the pond with a stick, string and worm, along with my cousins Rod and Shorty (Roger and Norma Jean to company). All we knew about fishing was, if you put a worm on a hook and sank it in the water, a fish might eventually come along and eat it. We didn't understand that exactly where in the water, let alone when, might make a difference.

Mostly we got little sunfish, and not too many of those. I know now that's because we mostly fished in the wrong places and because we usually did it in the middle of the day—at the worst possible time.

Leonard, of course, had the thing wired. He'd go out to the pond by himself and come back in an hour or so with enough big bass for supper. These were fish of a size and kind I'd never gotten myself, even though I'd spent a fair amount of time on the same pond. They also reinforced that suspicion that kept me from wanting to swim: the idea that there were things in the water you might not know about. I was astonished. Clearly, there was more to all this than I'd thought.

Leonard fished in the evenings when it was cool and the light was off the water, or sometimes at night when we kids were getting ready to go to bed. We assumed he went out then because that was when the work was finished.

Sometimes he used worms just like we did, but there were also minnows, crawdads, frogs, grubs, crickets and grasshoppers in evidence from time to time. He said that, yes, the kind of bait could make a difference, but added, "That ain't all there is to it."

Right, I could see that.

And sometimes he used these plugs with shiny metal scoops and blades on them and painted eyes and scales. Except for the dangling hooks, they had the bright look of toys. I liked them a lot but, although I could see they were supposed to be frogs or minnows, I couldn't believe a fish would actually mistake them for the real thing. Unless this was some kind of elaborate joke (which was always a possibility), Leonard must be right when he said, "Fish don't think like we do."

· · ·

EVENTUALLY, Leonard showed me how it was done, or, rather, he let me come along and watch and pick up what I could, provided I could keep quiet and stay more or less out of the way. He'd never lecture, but he'd try to answer whatever questions I felt like asking because the type of question would indicate how much information I was able to absorb. That way I didn't get confused and he didn't have to talk any more than was absolutely necessary.

Actually, Leonard was quite a talker most of the time, but on the water he'd go into a trancelike silence for long periods of time. Adults still tell kids to be quiet so they don't scare the fish, but that's not the real reason. It's just hard to explain to a child that a kind of profound physical and mental stillness is required if you want to catch fish. That's one of those things you have to come to on your own. Anyway, I learned not to chatter, and also to choose my questions well and ask them quietly.

Sometimes Leonard would pay me the supreme compliment of saying "I don't know" instead of making something up, although he could make up some great stuff when he was in the mood. If anything, I appreciate that even more now than I did then, but it still sticks in my mind as one of the first times an adult was honest with me.

There were some years in there when all I wanted to do in the summer was go see Uncle Leonard. That hung on for a while even after my family moved to Minnesota and there was some distance involved. The trips were fewer and farther between then, but they meant a ride on the Vista Dome Limited from Minneapolis to Chicago, a classy train from the days when people really traveled that way. These were my first long journeys alone, and if anyone asked I didn't say I was going to visit my uncle, I said I was going fishing. I was eleven or twelve years old by then and I felt pretty damned worldly.

I'd always gotten along with Leonard, but when my dad

and I eventually got into the normal bad times fathers and sons go through, I got interested in the difference between him and my uncle. It didn't occur to me until years later that the main difference was, one *was* an uncle and the other was a dad—two positions with very singular job descriptions.

I always felt like Leonard was telling me the truth as he saw it, while Dad was making what I now see as the classic mistake of telling me the world *was,* in fact, the way he thought it *should* be. The evidence for his position was not always compelling and there was a time when I thought my father was, if not a liar, then at least a propagandist.

Dad would sometimes tell me what I *would,* by God, do when I got older because that's what everyone did, while Leonard, when he said anything at all, tended to allow that I'd do what I thought was best when the time came.

The only limp advice Leonard ever gave me had to do with a girl I went to high school with whom I wanted to seduce. I don't remember exactly what he said, but it was seriously out of character: some kind of obligatory version of what he knew Dad would have said if I'd have dared to ask him about it, namely, "Keep it in your pants because everyone your age keeps it in his pants," even though we both knew everyone didn't. It was an awkward moment for both of us.

I finally realized that Dad was an idealist. I came to respect him for that in time, became something of an idealist myself and saw how that can make you impatient. On the other hand, Leonard once told me he didn't care if a guy was an idealist or a Presbyterian as long as he pulled his own weight. Interestingly enough, both of these guys were good fishermen.

IN later years I would come to understand the concept of sport, but a farmer in the Midwest of the 1950s had a somewhat different perspective on recreation. That is, he viewed everything he did as a chore, although he'd admit that some chores were more enjoyable than others. When he picked up his rod, Leonard would usually say something like, "Well, I guess I better go fishing" in the same tone of voice he'd use for "I guess I better get that tire changed."

The job here was to collect supper, and the only fish Leonard ever released ("threw back," that is) were the ones that were too little to keep. When he got as many as he wanted, he'd quit. To him, fish were a crop that just happened to be fun to harvest, and I think it delighted him to be able to cheat the work ethic that way.

To me, fun was fun, although when it was done in the company of an adult and the gratification wasn't immediate, there did seem to be a deeper meaning to it. There were these big fish in there that you could get if you did everything just right, and doing it right could be different today than it was yesterday. Furthermore, there were days when the adult couldn't figure it out any better than I could, and that gave me my first hint that I was not, in fact, stupid (as I often felt around grown-ups) but that the world was just a complex place where, as Leonard said, "Some days you get the elevator and some days you get the shaft."

Occasionally there were some very large bass. I won't try to guess at their size now because I was young and small then and this was a long time ago, but some of them were big enough to scare me a little, even though I still wanted them badly. The fine balance between those two emotions was delicious, and toothy fish like pike and big trout still do that to me. The rod, reel and line become not only instruments for catching fish, but also a way to keep some of these things at a safe distance until you can grab them just right.

It was one of those great mysteries that take hold of you early in life, and so I grew up to be one of those who, for better or worse, take their fishing seriously. Consequently, I got into fly-fishing, an area where considerations of sport come before those of practicality. I believe I stopped short of becoming a snob, though, and I think I owe that to farm ponds. These little puddles filled with panfish and surrounded by cows teach you early on that fishing is not necessarily a fine art.

F ARM ponds are a standard fixture in rural America, as ordinary and necessary as barns and barbed wire. You need water for the stock, so you dam a creek or dike up a swale to make a pond. In drier country you might have to sink a well and erect a windmill, or capture irrigation water. There's a science to this, not to mention volumes of water law. You have to know about drainages, soils and dike construction, and you have to be sure you actually have the rights to the water in the first place.

Here in the West, wars were fought over that kind of thing. They're still being fought, for that matter, but now people use lawyers instead of rifles, which makes it even nastier.

Once you had your pond, you naturally tossed some fish in it: probably bluegills and largemouth bass—the two most common warm-water farm pond fish in the U.S.— although other combinations have been known to work, too, and in cooler water you could stock trout. You did this because you were a farmer or a rancher and so you were in favor of self-sufficiency and against waste. This seems to be a genetic predisposition. There's something in the collective rural American consciousness that abhors a fishless body of water.

Some other things would probably arrive on their own in time: things like frogs, the eggs of which might be carried in stuck to the legs of herons. These birds might have dropped by the first year to see what was up and found a largely sterile body of water, although if they came back the next spring there'd be fresh tadpoles to eat.

Many of the aquatic insects would arrive under their own power, while cattail seeds, and maybe the seeds of some trees as well, came via the wind. No one knows where the bullheads came from, but they were always there. Someone once said the entire earth is covered with dormant bullhead eggs that hatch as soon as they get wet.

It's a case of what John Cole calls "natural persistence." We humans try to control things, but, for better or worse, the natural process moves in as soon as your back is turned to show you you're not entirely in charge.

Anyway, the dike was built, the water pooled and the organisms that liked it showed up in their own good time. To each new arrival, the place became irreplaceable overnight, as if it had been there for a hundred thousand years. And as long as a pond held water year-round, it would gradually soften at the edges and begin to go wild. A three-generation-old farm pond—one that has attracted cottonwood trees, ducks, muskrats and such—can be almost indistinguishable from a small, natural lake.

If you happened to enjoy fishing, a dock may have sprouted just as naturally, and sooner or later you'd probably barter yourself into a small boat of some kind. Not a bass boat or anything like that—you'd want a good, workable fish pond and a boat to match, but this was not what you'd call a big-ticket operation. All you needed was some old wooden scow that would stay afloat for a couple hours in the evening.

When the boat finally waterlogged and sank, you might have gotten a new one and left the old wreck on the bottom, planning to dispose of it properly when you got around to it. But there'd be lots of more important things to do, and in time the gunwales would become a faint outline down there in the weeds and muck. Given enough neglect the boat would finally dissolve altogether, saving you a couple hours of muddy work.

If you were like the farmers I remember from my child-hood, you wouldn't take the pond too seriously or get too fancy about it, but you'd probably manage it some in an effort to grow the biggest, healthiest fish possible. You might even go to the trouble of calling the County Extension Agent for advice and then buying some fish from a hatchery. Then again, that would cost money, so maybe you'd just catch a few bucketfuls of fish in another pond and haul them in, figuring if they took they'd be free, and if they didn't you wouldn't have wasted any money. Money was precious, but work was just work. There was an endless supply of it.

You'd fish the pond yourself when you had time, for kicks, a good free meal or both. Your kids, and maybe a young nephew, would catch their first fish there, and if you were a nice guy, you might let the occasional stranger fish it as well, if he asked nicely and looked okay.

T HAT's how most of us come to farm ponds as adults: We ask around or just knock on strange doors and humbly ask to fish. It doesn't always work, but if we're polite and don't look like mass murderers, it works often enough.

Maybe you spotted the pond while driving through farm country on your way somewhere else. There may have been fish rising in it, or maybe it just seemed right somehow. A good pond can have a certain look to it, although it's hard to describe exactly what that entails. Vegetation, shade and flooded trees are all good signs, but beyond that there's this kind of beckoning green warmth about it, like the collective auras of fifty largemouth bass hovering over the water. Whatever it is, it's sometimes possible to spot it in a split second at a thousand yards from the window of a speeding automobile.

I've known fishermen to do considerable research on farm ponds and private reservoirs, consulting county maps, aerial photos and tax records. Often people who go to that kind of trouble are looking for something to lease, but not always. Some of them are just hunting for something that's great because it's obscure, and they understand you can't see every farm pond in America from a public road.

Of course there are fishermen who won't look at farm ponds twice, probably because they're sometimes not very pretty as bodies of water go. These would be the same guys who go somewhere exotic, catch lots of huge fish in some lush wilderness, and then claim they're spoiled for anything less; people who have forgotten that, although fishing *can* be an adventure, it is basically just an ordinary, everyday aspect of a good life.

To me, it's the very homeliness of farm ponds that makes them so tantalizing. Some ponds are so well camouflaged that no one pays much attention to them, and so, when the conditions are right, populations of virtually wild fish can just percolate in there, growing larger and larger and not getting especially smart. In this way, a seedy little farm pond is more of a natural setting than a highly regulated catch-and-release trout stream.

IF you stay in one part of the country long enough, you might be able to develop a modest network of farm ponds that you can get on. You'll end up with some good, easygoing fishing close to home, and in private moments you can congratulate yourself for being cagey and connected in the finest tradition of the local fisherman. It'll help if you're not too shy about asking, and if you can accept rejection gracefully. It's a cardinal rule of farm ponds that if the man says no, then no it is, and he doesn't even have to explain why.

Now and then money will change hands (and I don't think money is dirty in this context), though often the exchange is something more personal, like some cleaned fish, or a six-pack.

This all fits in nicely with my personal vision of what a fisherman should be. He can be classy if he likes, but beneath that he's funky, rural, practical and not unacquainted with hard work. By that I mean, he may not actually *do* hard work, but he at least knows it when he sees it, which, in turn, means he knows enough to close the gates behind him without being told.

And, most of all, he's not entirely blinded by the scenery and the trappings. Sure, he can have a weakness for trout and big, pretty rivers, but if it's cows and chickens wandering

around the banks of the pond (rather than, say, mule deer
and blue grouse), then so be it. If the fish don't care, why
should he?

My friends and I will usually show up at a farm pond all
decked out for high sport with neoprene waders, belly boats,
fly rods, cameras: the whole thing. We remember when it
was different, but this is just how we do it now. We have
become fly fishermen.

Between us we carry fly patterns that imitate just about
any warm-water food organism you can name, plus those
goofy things that have what pass for anatomical features, but
that nonetheless look like nothing nature has ever produced
on this planet. After all, fish don't think like we do.

Sometimes we'll take the temperature of the water, someone usually knows what the barometer is doing at the moment and there may be talk of water chemistry, aquatic vegetation, moon phase, photo-periods as they relate to spawning
and feeding activity, insect migration patterns and so on.

Now and then the owner of the pond will be impressed.
More likely he'll be amused and a little puzzled, wondering
how we got it into our heads that anything, let alone fishing,
was that complicated.

2

TROUT
CANDY

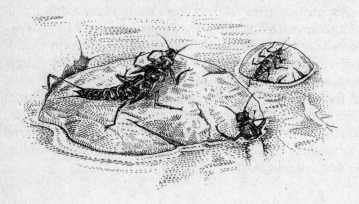

THE PHONE STARTED RINGING on Wednesday afternoon. The news had an urgent tone to it, but it was also vague. Either the willow flies were on over at the Colorado River and the fishing was great, or someone thought the flies *should* be on by now, or there was a third- or fourthhand report that they had been on a day or two ago. Something like that—something about the willow flies. This is how it usually begins.

The weather was damp and nasty—a low pressure front

was stalled over the northern Colorado Rockies—and I was down with a spring cold, or maybe a dose of the latest strain of flu, so I was slow to catch the enthusiasm.

My friend A.K. Best wanted me to drive over there with him on Thursday on the off chance there was some substance to the reports. In fact, he insisted on it. A.K., you see, is one of those guys who has actually fished this hatch in its glory. Like other fishermen in this same small fraternity, he claims he's never been quite the same since, so now he's a kind of evangelist for it.

He and Koke Winter hit it once sixteen years ago on the Big Hole River in Montana, and I've heard about it so many times now I can almost see it myself: the big flies flopping around on the surface of the river, the huge trout rising to eat them, the slurping of the fish audible over the background noise of the current. And the tip-off as these two men, then from Michigan, drove down the highway along the river: Some of the large, clumsy flies had formed up in an egg-laying flight over the road, thinking the black, shiny asphalt was water. They hit the windshield like sparrows.

The dry fly fishing that day had been, "Great . . . I mean, you know, *great.*" The story is well rehearsed by now, and these two guys are normally articulate, but on this subject they reach a point where words fail.

As cosmopolitan as fly-fishing has gotten in recent years, it still has some regional characteristics. Up there in Montana the bug in question is known as a stonefly, presumably because the nymphal form of the insect lives under large stones on the streambeds. (Large stones, but not small ones—no telling why.) In some other places the same bug is a salmon fly, possibly because of its body color. Here in Colorado it's the willow fly because the inch-and-a-half-long winged adults can be found hanging in those bushes along the river.

The big stoneflies spend almost all their lives (up to three years, which is long for a bug) as aquatic nymphs hunting and foraging along the bottoms of trout streams. They grow steadily, molt repeatedly and are regularly eaten by trout. In the right streams and rivers, a big stonefly nymph pattern fished near the bottom in deep water is the first thing most fly fishermen will try. Many large trout are caught this way.

Stoneflies are such a dependable and nutritious food source that a good stonefly stream is usually a good trout stream, too. The insects are also an indicator species for stream biologists. They need cold, clean, highly oxygenated water, and their presence means good water quality.

When a generation of stonefly nymphs reaches maturity they migrate to shallow water, climb out onto rocks, logs and bridge pilings, crack their nympha husks and hatch into winged insects. (Scientists say "emerge," while many fly fishermen still prefer "hatch." It's less accurate, but traditional.) After the bugs have mated, the females return to the stream, lay their eggs on the water and fall to the surface, spent. Many are then eaten by trout.

This would be every bit as poignant as the mayflies' well-known one tragic night of romance except that mayflies are delicate and pretty, while stoneflies are big and horrible. When they made that movie back in the 1950s where giant, radioactive grasshoppers took over the world, they missed a good bet by not using stoneflies instead. Next to a stonefly, a grasshopper looks cuddly.

Technically speaking (and fly fishermen can get annoyingly technical), there's more than one species involved here, but for all practical purposes it's the same insect: larger than a grasshopper; unattractive, even dangerous-looking; unpredictable in its habits and the ultimate in trout candy.

The sport of fly-fishing is grounded in the fact that trout feed primarily on insects, and the large members of the stonefly family are the biggest ones they ever see. Fish are said to go mad when the oversized flies are on the water. The biggest brown and rainbow trout in the river—the ones only bait fishermen ever see—are said to rise gaily to the surface like young sunfish. You can catch enormous trout on dry flies until your rod arm hurts. It's almost too easy, they say, although they always say that in an ironic tone of voice.

FLY-FISHING, you see, is supposed to be a very difficult and painstaking business in which success can be rare and fleeting and with complex philosophical undercurrents. That's the sport's main attraction and it's also the reason why so many of its practitioners are such misanthropes. We don't actually hate society, we just feel like we're plugged into something larger, better and more interesting, so that the more alienated we become on the one hand, the more at home we feel on the other.

Fishing is engrossing because it's so lovely, and that's central to everything. We try to be logical, but there's no way around it—we end up believing in whatever we think is beautiful, whether we can prove it makes sense or not. Everyone needs something wonderful in their life that they can't explain, and that they might not explain even if they could.

There's even a moral aspect. A fisherman—especially a fly caster who doesn't keep many fish—addresses the environment in what he feels is the only right way: not as a spoiler or an observer, but as a responsible participant who tries not to want much more than he honestly needs. It's easy to see how a guy like this could look at day-to-day life in America and begin to feel a little superior.

In fact, fishing *is* fairly difficult over the long haul. Success involves the exquisite timing of hitting the hatches just right, the foresight to have the right fly patterns and then at least some skill to take advantage of the situation. And, naturally, the best fishing is usually in the worst weather. Those of us who have stuck with it for a long time—catching some fish in the process—take pride in that.

We're also proud that this is a sport to which lives are dedicated. (We say "dedicated," others say "wasted" or even "pissed away.") Fly-fishing can be expensive and time-con-

suming; it induces fits of solitary contemplation and requires
a lot of travel, and, since most of the fish caught are released,
it seems like a strangely beautiful but otherwise pointless
thing to do: sort of like art. And, as with artists, there's a
mythology about the sacrifices and personal costs of being a
fly fisherman.

A friend tells this story about a fly fisher's wife: Before
they were married, the man told her, truthfully, "I don't
drink, take drugs, gamble or chase women, but I *do* fly fish."
Two years later the woman was heard to say, "It sounded
good at first, but now I wish he did some of those other
things instead." In the full context of the sport, stories of too
much fishing causing domestic trouble are better than the
ones where huge trout are either caught or lost. Remember,
this is all about belief, and without some suffering, both
physical and social, belief starts to look frivolous.

There are a few people around who still cling to that tired
old battle of the sexes routine where the men see fishing as
an escape from women and the women see it as a kind of
threat, but that really belongs to past generations who never
came to grips with passion. There's even a name for it now.
Dr. Don Powell of the American Institute of Preventative
Medicine recently defined the condition as psychosclerosis,
or "a hardening of the attitudes."

And, I should point out, the men who really do fish to
escape women don't fish at all, they drink and play cards.
Among most fishermen they are outcasts.

There are also some militant amateur headshrinkers
around who like to think you fish for dark reasons you don't
understand, but that they, of course, do. The rod is your
penis, the water is your soul and the fish are either God or
your mother. These are the people who will psychoanalyze
you at the dinner table whether you agree to it or not, and if
you *don't* agree to it, it's only because you're terribly re-
pressed.

I don't know, maybe there really are hidden chambers of

weirdness lurking beneath what seems obvious, but I think it's actually pretty simple. Fly-fishing is a healthy antisocial sport, and many of us have an emotional investment in being misunderstood because it makes us feel strange and brilliant, like Van Gogh.

Maybe that's why, when rumors of a stonefly hatch surface, we have this tendency to drop everything and drive hundreds of miles on the off chance that for once we can catch lots of big trout with almost no effort at all. We've paid our dues, we deserve it and, best of all, there are those who will never understand what all the excitement is about.

Those who've experienced it claim it does something to you. Exactly what it does is never clearly specified, but a good stonefly hatch has been compared to the first sexual encounter, or a religious conversion: one of those manifestations that reveal The Truth and make your previous life read like someone else's biography. And all this in aesthetic terms most people look askance at—slimy fish, nasty-looking bugs, icy water seeping into waders, etc.—which makes it the exclusive thrill of the true connoiseur.

Maybe a stonefly hatch changes you and maybe it doesn't. I *have* noticed that stonefly types have a kind of free-form intensity the rest of us lack: a kind of faith in something beyond reasonable expectations. These are the guys who would fish long and hard in the settling pond at a sewage treatment plant if that's all that was available. Like cats, they seem to see something the rest of us don't.

I don't know if it changed A.K. or not, because I met him after he'd hit the stonefly hatch in Montana. I can testify, however, that he's a little crazy now. Koke, too. Crazy and happy, which is the time-honored posture of the sport.

ANYWAY, A.K. insisted that I go over to the Colorado River with him on Thursday, but I said I couldn't because I was sick with a cold or something worse.

"The hell with being sick," he said. "This is important." There was something like indignant patriotism in his voice, as if I was trying to dodge the draft because of a hangnail.

"Sick!" I whined, "headache, runny nose, hacking cough, fever, depressed, no interest in sex: sick. I have no urge to drive halfway across the state and stand in an ice-cold river waiting for a hatch that never comes off anyway."

"Okay, but you'll be sorry," A.K. said.

There are a lot of western fishermen who know what I mean by that. I'm anything but a stonefly fanatic, but I'm familiar with the mythology, and in the course of things I have pursued these hatches off and on for fifteen or twenty years through four or five western states on the advice of people I probably shouldn't have trusted. I mean, what if your doctor or your banker had this insane plan with a slim chance of success and a look in his eye to match? Would you say, "Sure, whatever you think is best"?

I've been on the water before the hatch came off, and I've arrived just a day or two after it. I've even been there when the big flies were hanging in the bankside brush like mutant seedpods, but weren't on the water where the trout could eat them.

Sometimes there were other bugs around, good hatches of mayflies or caddis, and the fishing was great, but in the back of everyone's mind was the suspicion that it wasn't as great as it could have been.

I've fished flies imitating the nymphs ahead of the hatch and I've fished the dry flies after it. Trout have been caught, sometimes large ones, but for the mythic event itself I should have been there two days ago or I should stay another couple of days, because it's just about to happen. I've stayed. It's never happened. I carried the big dry flies in my box for so long the hooks rusted and I threw them away. Then I replaced them with new ones, just in case.

I like the big Bird's Stonefly pattern because it's an old-time western standard, and because it's quick and easy to tie.

There are newer, snazzier patterns around now because the big long-shanked hooks these things are tied on are the kind of large canvases fly-tiers like, but I can't see spending a lot of time at the vise on flies that are just going to rot away in the box.

A.K. and Koke left early Thursday morning, probably around four. They'd have been nearing the pass over to the Western Slope about dawn. I dragged myself up at nine—sniffling and moaning—had some coffee, skimmed some disturbing headlines in the morning *Rocky Mountain News,* then crawled back to bed and slept until near dark. I dreamed about paddling a canoe with great difficulty through deep shag carpet and woke up feeling like I was back from the dead. That is, I didn't feel great, but I felt better, as though maybe I'd live after all. I didn't really wish I'd gone fishing, but I did have the feeling that I'd wimped out.

The phone rang that evening.

"Well, we caught some fish, but it wasn't really happening. A few more days should do it. Let's go back on Monday."

The phone continued to ring over the weekend. The word was out, although it still wasn't clear what the word was. There were rumors, lots of contagious excitement, but no one had actually seen or fished the hatch.

As it turned out, A.K. and Koke went back on Monday ("It almost happened, but not quite. There were a few bugs in the bushes," A.K. said that evening) and I went up on Tuesday with Larry Pogreba and Ed Engle. I was still in a kind of weak, sick fog, but I had to go. This could be it. If I missed it I'd catch incredible grief from those who didn't. I was heavily medicated and at least ambulatory.

We drove to the river in Larry's souped-up vintage Cadillac, a fine luxury hot rod as big inside as an ambulance, with wide leather seats and electric windows. This thing is painted silver with tastefully pale pink-and-blue flames coming off the hood and front wheel wells. A radar detector is Velcroed to the dashboard.

It's a fast driver's car and Larry is a fast driver. He's even done it professionally, although those days—and those injuries—are now history. Still, fast driving becomes a way of life. Larry is a native westerner who grew up covering large pieces of empty real estate in record time. Out here that's a matter of homegrown practicality as well as something of a sport. His father was a fighter pilot, and it's been said of Larry that he "never quite has enough air under him."

We arrived at the town of Hot Sulpher Springs well ahead of schedule, having experienced only a low pucker factor. (The pucker factor—expressed as low, moderate or high—refers to the amount of upholstery a passenger sucks up his rectum due to fear.) We rigged up quickly and deployed along the river, Larry below the concrete bridge, Ed and I above.

Hot Sulpher is where current logic placed the advancing hatch. A day earlier, according to A.K., the bridge pilings were plastered with the dry nymphal husks of hatched stoneflies. After some wind and rain the previous night, Ed and I found only a few.

The day was gray, breezy and cool—even chilly if you were running a slight fever. It was early June, spring at that altitude, but it had been a dry winter, so the river was only a little off color. This, they were saying, was an excellent omen for the willow fly hatch, which sometimes comes off when the river is sand colored from runoff, making the big, luscious bugs all but invisible to the fish.

There were a few odd insects on the water—mayflies and caddis—and some trout rose sporadically here and there. We tried our big dry stonefly patterns first. It's said that trout like these bugs so much that once they've seen the real ones they'll hit the imitations for days after the hatch itself has petered out or moved on. We tried that, but it didn't work.

Then Ed tied on a dry caddis imitation and I tried the mayfly. Something to do while waiting for the main event.

Before long, Larry came by, fishing the way he drives, that is, hard. He was casting something large, dark and heavily weighted, probing all the deep holes where the trout should be, and he was moving. In ten minutes he'd disappeared around a bend upriver.

About then some kind of blue sports car peeled up on the dirt road along the far bank. Three guys piled out and began shaking and otherwise examining the bushes for willow flies. Nothing. Then they all stood for a minute watching Ed and me as we stood knee-deep in the river casting dry flies. They were all wondering what any fisherman wonders at a time like that, namely, "Are those guys oblivious, or do they know something we don't?"

Then they got in their car and drove off downstream in what would have been a cloud of dust if it hadn't rained the night before. Ed and I wondered if we should follow them, then decided against it.

By early afternoon we'd all caught a few fish using a variety of nymphs and dry flies. Larry and I had each turned very large trout that we'd seen and felt for an instant before they were gone. The rest of my fish were small, but a few in the foot-long range had been hot enough to take a little line. Ed landed a nice big rainbow on a little dry caddis fly. We were doing okay. Catching some fish.

We took a break then and walked over to Riverside Flys, a closet-sized fly shop in the basement of the Riverside Hotel. The proprietor's name was Ed Bennett. He looked a lot like Richard Brautigan.

The three of us stomped in in our waders, and I asked, "What's the story on the hatch?" No need to specify *which* hatch. Bennett looked up from the flawless stonefly nymph he was tying and said, "I don't know."

We dedicated a moment of silence to that, as people tend to do when confronted with the simple truth spoken plainly. The little room was crowded with all four of us in there. Behind the cluttered tying bench a few feathers and bits of fur were hanging on the wall in plastic bags. There was a case of flies, an easy chair and a strung-up fly rod leaning against the wall next to the open door. The distinctive aroma of wet neoprene waders was heavy. Outside, the river flowed by a few yards away. You could hear it gurgling.

Bennett said he'd fished up and down the river daily for the last few weeks. He'd seen a few willow flies, but not many. Maybe it was the cool, dank weather that made things slow. Who knew? It's a weird hatch under the best of conditions.

One thing was clear: Every day it didn't come off well brought it a day closer to never really happening at all. Sure, the bugs would get the business of mating, egg-laying and dying taken care of, and the trout would get a few good meals out of it, but the fishermen would come out feeling cheated, their corroding willow fly patterns stashed in the fly box for another season.

"That does happen sometimes," Bennett said.

Larry bought one of the perfect stonefly nymphs, and then we trudged up the block-long, mostly deserted main street to a bar where, Bennett had said, they probably wouldn't mind if we came in wearing our waders. They didn't. We ate wonderful homemade chili that was hot enough to momentarily clear my sinuses, and decided to hike downstream into the canyon for the rest of the afternoon. If it happened, we'd be there, if not, we were still fishing, right?

An elderly dachshund sat on the floor begging from me while I ate. I finally gave him a piece of tortilla, which he spat out.

The main street was drizzly and empty as we walked the block back to the river. There was one other man fishing on the water, an old guy casting a spinning rod without much enthusiasm.

In the bar there had been a hand-lettered sign on a door
saying, "Beds $6 a night—if you're too drunk to drive."
Good idea. I wished I'd peeked in there just to see how many
beds there were. Enough for the whole town, maybe. Hot
Sulpher is not large, and it's a place where the winters would
be long and grim.

W E got into rain gear and fished downstream. The canyon
starts to get steep and close in there, and it's big, deep water
for the mountains. You stand on the bridge and pick the side
you want to work down, figuring either way a lot of good
currents will be out of reach. This is a fact of life. On any
trout stream you can't cross, you'll be on the wrong side half
the time.

We examined the bankside willows for flies and didn't find
any, but the leaves were fresh, wet, lettuce green and shiny.
The bushes were full of yellow warblers that would flit out
over the water to catch small bugs and to alert observant
fishermen to the presence of trout food. Yellow warblers
would be too small to eat willow flies, but I wondered if they
were ever tempted to try.

We caught three or four small trout on nymphs, but we
never did see a winged stonefly, although there were a few
old nymphal husks around to show that they had, in fact,
emerged recently. Earlier, in the same place, A.K. and Koke
had seen a handful of flies in the bushes, but none on the
water, and no one we'd talked to had done any better than
that.

It was becoming clear that the hatch had come off without
us, but it was comforting to look at the few fragile husks that
hadn't dissolved in the rain yet and know it *had* happened.
At a time like this you congratulate yourself for being able to
appreciate beauty you haven't even seen, and you might
catch yourself thinking something like, I don't care what
anyone says, I am one sensitive son of a bitch.

It might also occur to you that this is why Old Faithful

geyser in Yellowstone is so popular with normal people: not because it's so spectacular, but because it keeps regular hours.

I know you've heard all this before, but stoneflies are just something a fisherman has to talk about. They're an old joke in a sport that leans toward triteness, but missing out once again on one of the great clichés of the sport is a cliché in itself, so it's okay.

I hadn't fully recovered yet, but I didn't feel too bad after that lunch. Mexican food does have some medicinal qualities. Still, during a coughing fit I wondered what my mother would say if she knew I was out fishing in the rain with a cold. Probably something like, "If you're no smarter than that by now, there's nothing more I *can* say."

3

THE
ROARING
FORK

THE ROARING FORK RISES at Independence Lake, 12,095 feet up in Colorado's Sawatch Range, and flows roughly northwest for 75 miles until it spills into the Colorado River at the mountain town of Glenwood Springs. I've always liked that term "rises." Something as neat as a river shouldn't just start, it should *rise*.

The Fork collects a handful of small creeks and two major

tributaries—the Frying Pan and Crystal rivers—and it has a steep gradient for most of its length, so it does, in fact, roar as it comes down out of the mountains. It also flows through what author and river-runner Jeff Rennicke has called "the most beautiful watershed in the state." That's a matter of opinion, but it is pretty, especially in those stretches where you look up the cottonwood-lined river and see the enormous bare crag known as Mount Sopris.

And, naturally, it holds trout: rainbows, browns, a few cutthroats, some brook trout in the higher reaches, as well as its share of mountain whitefish. If it wasn't for the fish, you'd be reading about the Fork in a book on kayaking.

A.K. and I had fished the Roaring Fork a time or two over the years, though never too seriously, and for several seasons we'd been telling ourselves we should give the river a proper and serious try. I mean, there it was, full of fish by all accounts, and we'd largely ignored it.

But, like many Colorado fly-fishing types, we have this thing for the nearby Frying Pan with its big trout, technical fishing and, by now, its comforting familiarity. It takes years to learn a river even slightly, and once you've done that you want to luxuriate in it for a while.

We'd always look at the Roaring Fork on our way up to the Pan—you drive by a long stretch of it between Glenwood Springs and Basalt—and there was always that feeling of a lost opportunity, especially on the way out after spending several days in that country and, once again, never quite getting around to the Fork.

I think it had something to do with the river's proximity. It was right there, and whenever we were in the area we could fish it anytime we wanted. Consequently, we hardly ever did. A.K. once said, as we drove past it again, that if the thing was 500 miles away in another state we'd have already spent a week on it.

And, if the truth were known, we were a little intimidated by the Fork. For one thing, it's a big, brawling stream—a major tributary of the Colorado, but also a damned impressive river in its own right. It is fast and filled with slick, cannonball-sized boulders, so it can be tricky to wade even with cleats and a staff. The quick, braided currents can make a dry fly drift difficult, and it's large enough that much of the water remains out of reach to wading fly casters. Even in the low flows of September, that far bank—the one that's in shade, where all the fish are rising—might as well be in the next county.

And then there are the access problems, which are many and various. There's a fair amount of well-known (if not always well-marked) public water on the Roaring Fork, but parts of it are a patchwork of private property and private arrangements that are probably best not messed with if you don't already know the river well or have a reliable local source.

The official word goes like this: From McFarlane Creek above the town of Aspen downstream to upper Woody Creek Bridge (a stretch of about 15 miles) the regulations are flies and lures only, catch and release. Walt Burkhard of the Colorado Division of Wildlife estimates that roughly half of that is open to the public, with leases and private water scattered throughout. "Of course, that's just a guess," he said, "I don't have my maps in front of me."

From the bottom of the catch-and-release area down to the confluence with the Colorado River the rules are flies and lures, with a bag limit of two trout 16 inches or longer. Burkhard says this additional 15 miles or so is virtually all controlled by ranchers who, under Colorado's open range law, do not have to post their land for it to be legally considered private. Some of these landowners will let you on, some of them won't, and, as every fisherman knows, this can change from season to season if not from day to day. The word locally is, you can get on the water, but sometimes it takes a little research.

There are always two sides to these kinds of access complications. It's true that you can't always fish exactly where you want to, but, on the other hand, the trout are not

spooked, hook-scarred, overeducated or otherwise hammered into submission, and the water never seems to be
crowded. Actually, when you get a good view of it from the
road, it always looks blissfully empty.

A.K. and I knew of only a few spots where we could get
on the Roaring Fork, including a fine whitefish hole where
we would sometimes go to collect the fresh main ingredient
for a pot of cioppino. In contrast to the special regulations on
trout, there is no bag limit for whitefish, so you can fill a
washtub with them if you want to. There are those who do
that and no one seems to mind.

We'd fish a #8 golden stonefly nymph with a big dark
stone on a dropper, dredging the deeper, calmer pools the
whitefish like. Sometimes one of us would accidentally hook
a large trout, although we were often too surprised to land it.
Still, we had this picture of the Fork as a whitefish river with
a few trout in it, so, although we heard tantalizing things
about it from time to time, I guess we never quite took it
seriously.

T HE first time I fished the Fork was with Koke. That was
early in the season over a decade ago. I'd heard about it, but
that was about all. Koke claimed there were great big trout,
however, and he was said to know about such things.

The water was high and a little off color that day. We
drove up the river, stopping here and there, looking for the
big dark stoneflies that never quite materialized that year, or
any year since that I know of. I remember parking in what
looked to me like driveways, hopping some well-maintained
barbed-wire fences and otherwise getting on water that most
of us would assume was private. None of it was actually
posted, nor did anyone seem to be at home in any of the
nearby houses.

But Koke knew the river. In fact, he's famous around here
for knowing rivers and for being on a first-name basis with
anyone in Colorado, Wyoming or Montana who has any-

thing whatsoever to do with a trout stream, though he's also famous for not saying much about what he knows. I assumed he had permission, and in a pinch I figured I could point to him and say, "He told me it was okay, arrest *him.*"

I guess, in retrospect, the whole thing made me a little nervous. We didn't catch many fish, saw no stoneflies at all and it was starting to look like just another one of those stonefly hatch wild-goose chases in the company of another one of those nuts saying, "Well, it's not happening right now, but you should see it when it *does* happen."

I finally convinced Koke we should go over and try the Frying Pan, where we did well on a Blue-winged Olive hatch.

The answer, clearly, was to float the river with someone who knew its legal and fishy ins and outs, and we did that a few days before the Fourth of July weekend one summer with Tim Heng, fishing guide and then-manager of the Roaring Fork Anglers in Glenwood Springs. Tim, like a dozen other people, had told us that the Fork was a real good trout stream, and he felt it was being unfairly overshadowed by the Frying Pan, where all the *yuppies* fished. So we put his Mackenzie boat in somewhere around Carbondale and spent the day floating the roughly 15 river miles down to the confluence of the Roaring Fork and Colorado.

And it *was* the answer, at least in terms of a formal introduction to the river: the Montana-style, fast-paced, big-water assault where you get one cast per spot, and then your line is in the air as you look downstream for the next place that ought to hold a fish. You're on a wide, navigable river, but for the most part you're fishing a two- or three-foot-wide strip along one bank or the other. By the end of the day your arm is sore, there are the beginnings of blisters on your casting hand and you've caught a large number of trout, although you can't actually remember how many because it all seemed to happen so fast. You probably didn't even take many photographs, because you were too busy.

If you're not careful, you can get pretty cranked up

and continue the same pace off the water. You quickly load the boat onto the trailer, pack your gear, race back to camp, build a fire, slap something together for supper and then, with a plate of stew on your lap, you think, Wait a minute . . .

IN case you've never been in one, a Mack boat is a fine river craft. It's roomy, comfortable, stable and highly maneuverable in the right hands; the kind of boat you immediately feel at home in. It's also handsome, with a nice hint of the dory about it, and it's made for fishing, so everything is pretty much as it should be.

I do like casting from one of these things, especially when I can stand in the bow with my knees locked in those leg braces some of them have that make you feel like part of the boat, but mostly I like to use a float boat as transportation to otherwise inaccessible spots along the river where you can get out and wade.

You fish from the boat, of course (how could you just sit there with a rod in your hand?), but what you're really looking for are those tempting runs where you can get out and fish carefully for half an hour, read the water, look at bugs, maybe locate a difficult trout that takes twenty well-considered drifts and three fly changes to hook.

We did some of that, but the fact is much of the Roaring Fork must be fished from the boat or not at all. There are steep canyon walls and/or tall trees crowding the banks in many spots—no place to beach the boat, and if you did get out you'd be standing in the spot you should be casting to. And, of course, much of it is private. It's hard to tell from out on the water, but the guides know.

Fishing from a moving Mackenzie boat isn't exactly contemplative, but it's great fun, especially when you hook a big fish in fast water, the boat goes one way and the trout goes another. At one point I even had a heavy fish yank the rod out of my hand, something I'd heard of but had never actually seen before. I saved the rod, the fish broke off and A.K. laughed so hard he blew half a dozen casts, which served him right. Tim chuckled politely, but managed to keep his oars in the water.

I also want to say, without getting too mushy about it, that Tim Heng is one of the best boatmen I've ever been out with. It was one of those rare times when something just short of telepathy was going on between the guide and the sports. He seldom had to say "Good spot coming up on the right" and we never had to ask "Could you get a little closer here?" It went smoothly, there was little conversation, trout were caught. There were moments when we were functioning as a single unit with two oars, two fly rods and three heads. The mood was broken only occasionally when, for instance, some klutz dropped his rod.

THE Roaring Fork is a fast freestone river, so much of the fishing has a rough, western texture to it. In the morning, under a hot, sunny sky, we fished large Coachman Trude dry flies with peacock-bodied nymphs on droppers: attractor-style rigs that work in big water. Usually the trout would hit the nymph, and the white-winged Coachman Trude—acting as a bobber—would sink authoritatively, although a fish would take the dry fly just often enough to keep you on your toes.

The preferred underwater pattern here is the Prince Nymph, but a Zug Bug or even the peacock and partridge soft hackle I was using will pass nicely: anything in about a size 12 with a peacock herl body.

The Coachman Trude is the dry fly Tim recommends, but he allows that various other buoyant, white-winged patterns will also work. Trout, like people, eventually take on some of the characteristics of their environment, and in a brawling river like this, most of the fish are eager and grabby when they're feeding, so you use a big fly that you, and they, can see.

Later in the day the sky went from brilliant blue to a
bright, aluminum-colored overcast and some big Green
Drake mayflies began to emerge. This is an enigmatic hatch
on the Roaring Fork, but it's one we'd scheduled the float in
hopes of catching.

When we asked Tim about it, he said, yes, the hatch could
be on, it was time, conditions seemed right and some fishermen had even reported seeing the big mayflies. "We might
just hit it," he said, "you definitely want to have the flies."

That's what we wanted to hear: the careful "maybe if
we're lucky." If a fishing guide ever gives you anything that
sounds like a guarantee, you know he's about to be punished
for his arrogance, and you'll be in the boat with him when it
happens.

Green Drakes are considered to be one of the best
hatches in the West and they can attract lots of fishermen,
but the Drake hatch on the Roaring Fork is still largely
unspoiled because it's spotty, unpredictable, it moves
around a lot and it can be hard to follow through water that's
rough and sometimes private. After quite a few years of
talking to people over there, I can say many more people
know about it than have ever fished it.

Being normal twentieth-century fly fishers, we switched to
Drake patterns after seeing the first bug on the water. Later
I wondered if a big attractor dry fly like a Royal Wulff would
have worked just as well (Tim said it wouldn't have surprised him if it had), but we never thought to try it at the
time. Something like a Wulff might have helped because, on
big, fast water in dull light, even a big fly is hard to see when
it's tied in shades of steely olive and gray.

I'm curious, but I'm not complaining. You just always
wonder about things like that: You did well, but maybe you
could have done even better. As it was, we caught some big
trout.

.   .   .

A BIG fish on the Roaring Fork is as comparative a concept as it is on any other river. In one long day we landed a few trout that were under 10 inches, a few more that were hovering around 18, with the rest in between. Our best fish were taken below the confluence with the Frying Pan at the town of Basalt where the river is larger, in the two-fish-16-or-over stretch.

Sixteen-inch and larger trout are not uncommon in this water except, Tim said, when he has clients who want to keep some fish. Then, suddenly, most of them seem to run about 15½.

And the really big trout do turn up on something like a regular basis. Every time I've been in the area people are talking about the current hog from the Roaring Fork. Usually it's a brown, now and then a rainbow. You hear numbers like 7 pounds, or 9 pounds, and sometimes the guy telling the story holds out his arms as if he were about to grab a refrigerator.

Tim said the Roaring Fork is mainly a caddis river (that would be the bushy Elk Hair Caddis in various sizes or down-wing attractor patterns), but there are some other interesting hatches, too. Pale Morning Duns and Blue-winged Olives in April, and the big dark stoneflies that may or may not come off around the end of May or early June. The less glamorous but more reliable golden stoneflies should be on about the same time.

The Green Drakes are around for only about two or three weeks toward the end of June or early July. They're best on cloudy days.

The fishing tends to slow down a bit through August and much of September when the water is warm (although the evenings can be good) and then it picks up again in late September/early October with streamer fishing for big spawning browns that can run as late as mid-November.

Winter fishing is spotty, and the whitefish bite best and have the firmest meat in February.

That was the practiced recitation so many guides deliver so well over shore lunch: the capsule natural history of a river from a sporting point of view. It was backed up by the realities of the business—the booking schedule of the guides and the bins of fly patterns back at the shop—and, given the vagaries of trout fishing, it will all work. But, naturally, it's not all there is.

At the end of it Tim smilingly allowed as how there were a few other minor odds and ends he could mention, although he didn't, and A.K. gave me one of those looks over the rims of his prescription polarized bifocals. We understood that under the heading "minor odds and ends" you'll find, among other things, those few 7- to 9- pound trout. We also understand that the guide who doesn't keep a little something for himself (and maybe for the occasional client of a lifetime) is probably simpleminded.

I mentioned the business angle because I think it makes a difference from both the guide's and the sport's point of view. I like to think that if Tim didn't make his living at this (and still knew what he knows) he'd be saying, "Sure, there are some trout in the Fork, but it's basically a whitefish river," and A.K. and I would be watching his face for the tic in the mouth or the glint in the eye that would reveal that statement to be bullshit.

So, in the afternoon we caught fish on Green Drakes, with the big long-shanked size 12 flies looking like #20 Blue Duns on the big water. In the few miles where the hatch was actually on, we stopped or slowed down often to cast to rising trout, many of which were working away from the bank in the faster currents we could never have reached from shore.

When we finally drifted out of the stretch where the Drakes were hatching, Tim told us to keep fishing with the same flies, at least for a while. The hatch had already moved through this lower water, he said, so the trout should have fresh memories of what a Green Drake looks like.

They seemed to. With one exception, we fished Drake patterns all the way down to the Colorado and the fish seemed to know exactly what they were supposed to be.

Through one short stretch a nice little hatch of Pale Morning Dun mayflies was coming off. We had time to change flies and get a few casts over the rising fish, but this was one of those places where we could float through, but were not allowed to set foot on the bank or the bottom. Seventy-five yards of that—with Tim straining to slow the boat against the current—and we were back to happily banging the banks with the Drakes.

If there's anything wrong with fishing like this it's that you don't see enough of the river. That is, you see a strip of rock and water unrolling along the bank, which is pretty enough, but not nearly all there is to it. Now and then you'll glance up to see red rock cliffs, gray rocks with rosettes of lichen, groves of cottonwoods, patches of wildflowers, sagebrush-covered hillsides, pastures, a barbed-wire fence, a ranch building, a blue heron, the occasional cool, green grotto with the songs of warblers echoing out of it.

Through an especially good stretch where the trout were big and we were getting strikes on every cast, I looked around to try and figure out where we were—you know, for future reference—but it was pretty much useless. We were in a spot somewhere on the river that was probably private and that would take weeks to find again on foot.

Best to just catch a few of these trout before we drift downstream and it's all lost for what might as well be forever. The first time on new water all you really do is catch a few trout and learn whether you need to come back, maybe to spend years there in increments of two days to a week.

That night in camp I suggested to A.K. that maybe a truly dedicated outdoor journalist should float the river a second time and just watch the scenery to get a proper feel for the landscape, wildlife and other deep background stuff.

"Fine," A.K. said, "you watch, I'll fish."

That sounds like the comment of your typical balls-to-the-wall, catch-'em-all-or-die-trying kind of fly fisherman, and A.K. does usually fish with what appears to be complete patience and perfectly focused concentration. Still, he notices things I don't, even though between us I'm more likely to be the bank-sitter and bird-watcher.

After a fast-paced float like this, during which I saw very little that wasn't right in front of me, he'll ask, "Did you see those deer, those ducks, that golden eagle, that log barn?" and I'll have to say, "Uh, no. Where was that?"

W E floated into early evening. The river got wider and a little slower in places, and I found myself casting with the rocking motion of the shoulder I fall into when I'm getting bushed.

I honestly don't know how many trout we caught. Dozens, plenty, more than enough, more than we deserved. We caught so many that toward the end we were a little dazed by it all and I, for one, was just going through the motions and thinking simple, one-syllable thoughts like "yes," "trout," "good," "tired."

I still didn't know where we were, but then I glanced up and saw a middle-aged guy in white shoes sitting in a lawn chair, sipping what looked like a gin and tonic. That had to mean we were within the city limits of Glenwood Springs and it was almost over. The man looked right at us with a neutral expression and didn't wave.

He had a nice place there, with the property sloping down to the river, but he wasn't a fisherman. A fisherman would have either shook his head or raised his glass.

4

THE
FAMILY
POOL

THE FAMILY POOL IS IN THE CHEESMAN CANYON stretch of the South Platte River in Colorado. This is an old favorite fishing spot of mine—the pool in particular and the canyon in general—so I naturally thought about trying to disguise it here. That sort of thing is entirely permissible when writing about fishing as long as you don't get too cute or too superior about it.

I considered it, but then realized that in this case I didn't have to worry about revealing the spot. After all, this particular section of the Platte is a kind of showpiece trout river. It has been designated by the Division of Wildlife as a Gold Medal stream, and by the U.S. Fish & Wildlife Service as an irreplaceable, class 1 fishery; it is the state's oldest and best-known catch-and-release area (to hold up your end of an angling conversation in Colorado you have to have fished it), and the fight over the proposed Two Forks Dam project has brought it to regional, if not national, attention.

In old newspapers you can find photos of various dignitaries and celebrities who have fished the canyon or, more likely, the water below it that's easier to get to. President Bush has never fished it, but I know he's been invited.

Some years ago a friend of mine sent an article on Cheesman Canyon to a national outdoor magazine and the editor wrote back, "Christ! Don't you guys in Colorado fish anywhere else?"

In other words, it's a famous river, and I guess I'd have trouble referring to it as "a pretty good trout stream somewhere in the Rockies" with a straight face.

In a part of the country known for pretty canyons, Cheesman is an unusually handsome one. It's steep sided, narrow, deep and raw looking, with sparse stands of spruce and pine where it isn't littered with fabulously huge, lichen-covered granite boulders that have come loose and plowed their way down from the canyon walls.

I have never gotten used to the size of these rocks. You're supposed to feel insignificant when you look at something like the night sky, but what does it for me is something more immediate, like a lopsided pile of five boulders, each one bigger than my house.

The stream stair-steps down through this in riffles and smooth, green pools, making some of the most luxurious pocket water you'll ever see. A series of fishermen's trails

now run the length of it, but there are places where the
footing is skimpy and dizzying, especially in those spots
where the trail leads you high above the river and the gravelly scree that passes for soil wants to crumble away under
your feet.

From those vantage points—on days when the light is
good and the wind is down—you can usually spot fish in the
pools, although you learn that when conditions are such that
you can see them, they are damned hard to catch.

The Family Pool itself is near the bottom of the canyon.
When you hike in on the Gill Trail and begin to work your
way upstream, it's about the sixth obviously good hole you
come to. I could tell you to look for the big rock, but that
probably wouldn't help much.

I don't know for sure how it got its name, but I have a
theory: The pool isn't properly a pool at all like some of the
other placid holes in the canyon, but more of a braided run
at the end of a long riffle. Trout feed well in the faster water
there, and the current helps to mask flies that are a little too
big, not to mention slightly sloppy casts and drifts that are
less than absolutely perfect. When you're standing on the
trail above it, the Family Pool is one of the places where you
usually *can't* spot trout, even on a bright, calm day. Relatively speaking, it's an easy spot to fish, and I think people
used to bring their families there so the kids could catch
something.

That would have been in the old days when you could kill
trout. It's rare to see a family in the canyon anymore. Now
it's mostly serious grown men dressed from the better cata-
logs.

It would also have been in the old days that you could have
legitimately called the Family Pool—or any other spot in the
canyon—"easy." Even before the no-kill rule, a lot of canyon
regulars released all their trout, and the fishing got progres-
sively more difficult in the years after the regulations went
on, finally leveling out at what I guess must be the upper
intelligence level of your average trout. You can still catch

them—and sometimes you can do very well because there are a lot of fish in there—but you cannot make many mistakes. The fishing has been described as "highly technical," and beginning fly fishers have been heard to say they don't think they're ready for the canyon yet.

I know what they mean by that because I wasn't ready the first time, either. I had more or less learned to catch trout with a fly rod, and had reached that first plateau where you begin to think, This is not as hard as some people make it out to be. Then, after the first few times I sauntered into the canyon—the picture of confidence with store-bought flies and freshly patched waders—I had to admit that maybe it could be pretty damned hard after all, and frustrating, too, because the fish were big and you really wanted them.

I stayed with it, though, and eventually started to catch trout there. I had to because it's a rite of passage. Around here, if you don't crack the canyon, it will be said that you never really got serious about fly-fishing. My first few trout in the canyon were from the Family Pool, up at the head of it in the fast water where a good old Adams dry fly would pass for the more accurate Blue-winged Olive mayfly dun I later learned to use in the slower water.

I guess the Family Pool was the first spot in the canyon where some of my friends and I actually gained some purchase on what was then the hardest trout fishing we'd ever tried to do. It was also the first place we learned to put a name to. A passing fisherman told us what it was called back when there were few enough other anglers that you could stop and talk to them.

We got into the small, entomologically accurate fly patterns everyone said you needed (nothing bigger than a size 18) and began carrying boxes of tiny nymphs, floating nymphs, emergers, thorax duns, stillborns, no-hackles, parachutes, and so on.

Those of us who weren't into it already took up fly tying because we couldn't afford to buy all this stuff. Then we began to argue about whether the trailing nymphal husk on an emerger pattern should be wood duck flank or dun hackle tip. We also worked on our casting a little bit and began carrying spools of 7x tippet material.

This is where we began to realize that successful trout fishing isn't a matter of brute force or even persistence, but something more like infiltration. Technique is part of it, but so is keeping your head straight and your touch light. We were proud of our successes and became philosophical about them. This was about the time when we all started saying "Fishing is like life," which of course it is.

For years we'd head to the Family Pool first because—if things were right and no one was on the water ahead of us—it was usually good for a couple of fish. Hooking a few right off the bat would wire us up for the rest of the day and we'd eventually wander off to other spots that we came to know as the Wigwam Pool, the Ice Box, The Channels, The Flats, The Spring Hole, The Chute, The Holy Water—and to a few other places that I really *am not* going to tell you about.

Still, when A.K. or Ed or Jim Pruett or I would go down there in separate cars, all we'd ever have to say was, "I'll meet you on the river," without having to specify the Family Pool.

Another nice thing about the Family Pool is that it fishes pretty well in most stream flows, except for the very highest when it becomes the Family Rapids. There are a lot of spots in the canyon that fish nicely in one kind of flow, but not so well in others. I don't have a problem with that. In fact, it's fun to be able to look at how high the river is and sort of figure where you might be able to catch some fish. But it's also handy to know of a place that will probably be good no matter what—as long as you can get to where you have to be on it.

When you come into the canyon you are on the north side of the river, but if you want to fish the Family Pool you need to be on the south bank. Trust me on this, I've tried it both ways. On the north bank you are standing among the fish and it just won't work.

In normal flows, there are two places to cross the river in this stretch; one below the pool and one above. When the river is running high, it's best to try crossing at the wide riffle upstream. A good wading staff helps. I learned one spring, after nearly drowning, that if the wading is too tense there, then the pool is too high to fish well anyway.

And when the Family Pool is too high to be good, you probably should have gone to a different river or maybe to a farm pond for some bluegills.

I KNOW that I first fished the canyon in 1974 because that was three seasons before the catch-and-release regulations went on. That would be eighteen years, two wives and six jobs ago now. Technically, this makes me a veteran: a guy who remembers it from "before"—the main difference between then and now being the number of people. You naturally enjoy this old-timer status, and glorifying the old days a bit seems unavoidable. I do remember when there were more 18- and 20-inch trout in there, but, honestly, there was never a time when they were *all* 20 inches.

The size of the trout and their numbers have fluctuated over the years and there have actually been some poor to mediocre seasons, although, to be fair, even then the trout in Cheesman Canyon are a little bigger and some prettier than most around here.

There are those who say the decline had to do with poaching, while others claim it was the fault of the people at the Denver Water Board who do damaging things with the stream flows at crucial times of year. When we're not trying to address them politically, some of us think of the Water Board as a malevolent natural force—the modern equivalent of evil spirits.

The fisheries biologists I've talked to aren't sure, but they won't rule out the stresses on the fish from continuous, heavy fishing pressure or even natural population cycles. Or, for that matter, all of the above plus some other things we don't know about.

The last time I was down there it seemed to me there were fewer trout than in recent years, but some of them were bigger. And so it goes.

A lot of new fishermen began to show up when the no-kill rule went on, and we learned, along with the Division of Wildlife, that enlightened regulations can be even more glamorous than good fishing. In this context, there are two extreme kinds of anglers. Some just don't fish a place until it becomes fashionable, while a few others slink away the minute it does. In the long run, there are always more of the former than the latter.

Most of my friends and I fall somewhere in the middle. We bitch about the crowds and have taken to fishing the canyon on weekdays at weird times of the year, but we keep going back, even though now there are people on the water we don't recognize—not so much the individuals as the type.

For instance, there are the guys who carry those pocket counters in their vests. Ask one of them "Are you doing any good?" and he'll whip the thing out and say, "I have taken 27 fish since nine this morning. That would be an average of 6.75 trout per hour."

"Ah . . ." you say, for lack of a better response.

When we started fishing the canyon together, my friends and I saw the catch-and-release business as more mysticism than game management—an attitude that I know aggrieves some fisheries biologists who just don't see the religious implications of it. And there was also something in there about an enlightened lack of competitiveness that would eventually lead us into harmony with ourselves and the environment. We gave this some thought at the time, or at least we directed a lot of talk at it.

Eventually that mellowed to the kind of perspective the Division of Wildlife guys might agree with. You hike in and fish hard and as well as you can. At the end of the day when you climb out of the canyon, you're refreshed from the "quality Colorado outdoor sports experience," but you're empty-handed, however well you did. Having to release any trout you catch means—in an odd sort of way—that it doesn't matter if you catch any or not.

But of course it *does* matter if you catch fish or not. It's a paradox, and as any fisherman knows, one good paradox can cancel out hours of idealistic wrangling.

You can get better at fishing as time goes by (simply getting better is probably the ultimate goal of the sport), but there's a moment when your ideas about it set up and become more or less permanent. Then you spend the rest of your active life trying to balance the way things should be with the way they are. Maybe it has more to do with your age than anything else. I know a number of people whose thoughts on sport solidified—for better or worse—in their early to mid-thirties, and that was that.

I think my own glowing vision took shape sometime after I began to catch trout on dry flies in the Family Pool on a fairly regular basis and felt ready for more difficult water and a bamboo fly rod. On film that vision would resemble a trout-fishing documentary starring Thomas McGuane, written by Russell Chatham and directed by Akira Kurosawa. You're not aware of this kind of thing when it happens, but in retrospect you come to know that it occurred while you were knee-deep in a certain pool on a certain river in September of 1979. You were fishing a #18 Blue-winged Olive emerger on a 5-weight fly rod that you no longer own.

So the Family Pool has become a kind of focal point for some of us. In a way it reveals more about our feelings for all this than water we fish more often because it's always an event. The place is only a two-hour drive and then a short hike from here, but weeks and even months go by when we don't get down there. Still, this is the best trout water any of us fish on a regular basis. It's a treat; a homecoming; also a

trip where you take one of your very best bamboo fly rods.
When we fish it we're on our best behavior, that is, we're
about as serious, careful and patient as we ever get.

IT also comes up in conversation a lot. On a cool, overcast
day in March, someone is likely say out of the blue, "This
would be a good time to be fishing the Family Pool," and
then someone else will pick it up. "The flow will be about
300 cubic feet" (probably lower, actually, but we're fantasiz-
ing now) "and a midge hatch will be on. Or maybe the
mayflies are starting." There's a moment of silence then as
we all visualize it. This exchange usually takes place in town,
although it's even been known to happen on another trout
stream if the fishing is slow.

Don't get me wrong, the fishing can be slow in the Family
Pool, too. Because of the crowds in the summer, we now fish
it mostly in what some think of as the off season—roughly
from October to late March or early April—which would
include the late and the early Blue-winged Olive hatches,
with midges in between. It can be cold then, and there's an
ancient stone fire ring on the south bank where—I like to
think—generations of fishermen have built willow-twig fires
for warmth and coffee while waiting for the trout to start
rising. The fishing can be surprisingly good between fall and
spring, but the hatches can be spotty, and patience is often
called for.

I also like to think that if this old, blackened fire ring
wasn't already there when we discovered the place, we'd
have built one ourselves. This is a good pool that's worth
waiting out, and it's also a friendly, domestic sort of spot that
encourages coffee breaks, conversation and the occasional
deep thought.

I think it was there that I finally decided to quit smoking,
even though I know I'll always dearly love the drug, and
even though I didn't tackle the job that very day. It wasn't
the constant harping from the Surgeon General that did it,

or the pointed suggestions of friends, or even the fact that the
whole culture is encouraging tobacco heads to kick. The fact
is, I've never responded well to criticism. The more people
told me I shouldn't do it, the more I thought, It's a free
country, I'll smoke if I want to.

What it was, finally, was the realization that I am a plod-
ding worker and a slow learner and it's going to take a long
life for me to enjoy the few things I'll ever figure out. That,
I suppose, is the kind of thing that comes to you on the bank
of a difficult, but familiar trout stream—not to get sentimen-
tal about it or anything.

And there's been some serious talk around that fire, too.
Up until recently a lot of it had been about the proposed Two
Forks Dam project that, if built, would have flooded much
of the river. Not long ago the Environmental Protection
Agency, after many delays, finally came out with a final veto
of the project. Oddly enough, those of us who had opposed
the thing for years didn't buy champagne and celebrate. I
think we were a little numb, feeling less like we'd won a
battle and more like we'd just narrowly escaped getting hit
by a truck.

So lately the talk has been turning to how good it is to have
the canyon back. (It did seem for a while as if we'd already
lost it.) Of course it doesn't stop there. There seems to be an
unlimited supply of persistent, hard-hearted bureaucrats out
there, and the pouting water providers who've been deprived
of their project are now saying the new dams that will have
to be built will cause even more environmental damage than
Two Forks would have. It's an undisguised threat that, I
suppose, sets the tone for the next fight.

But until that fight shapes up, we can't seem to leave Two
Forks alone. The party line had been to defend the canyon
and the miles of water below as pristine wilderness, although
water providers who did their homework—not to mention
habitual devil's advocates like Ed—pointed out that the
fishery in question is actually somewhat artificial.

Releases from the existing dam at the head of the canyon

keep water temperatures more or less uniform and create a tailwater fishery, or a kind of man-made spring creek. Wasn't it a little paradoxical to have been fighting to save a stretch of river from a dam when said river was *created* by a dam?

Well, no, I'd tell Engle. A thing's origin in the past (going on a century in the past in this case) doesn't have anything to do with its quality in the present. And the sketchy historical info indicates this was a pretty good fishing stream even before Cheesman Dam, although it was cutthroats then instead of browns and rainbows. And the canyon still *looks* exactly like it has for a million years.

Goddammit, Ed, I know you agree with me on this!

But to Ed, arguing is a sport, sometimes even a contact sport, and to an outside observer our friendship would look like a running rhubarb that's been going on for almost twenty years now. The point he's making is valid, though: Isn't it interesting that the logic you apply to the opposition is abrupt and unforgiving, while the reasoning for your own position is fluid, creative and finds room for infinite subtleties?

About then someone sees a trout rise—or thinks he does—and everyone watches the water. Sure enough, a couple of fish have begun working down in the tail of the pool. Okay, who's going to try for them first? And what do you suppose they're feeding on?

No one goes out of his way to make this point, but it's another good one: You must be an environmental activist at some level—there's no way around it that'll still let you live with yourself—but you should never get so grim about it that you stop enjoying what you're supposed to be fighting for. Even if you lose in the end and some consortium of bastards dams the river, it won't be because you didn't speak up. And for the moment at least, you are still living in the good old days.

I MOVED West in the late 1960s and have lived around Colorado ever since. Montana, with bigger rivers, fewer people and harder winters, beckons occasionally, but I guess I like it here well enough. For some reason, I finally settled on the outskirts of Lyons, a town that's roughly the same size as the little Illinois burg where I was born.

Small towns are all the same. I lived here a long time before there were any signs of acceptance, and when they came they were not in the form of a parade down Main Street. Some people tentatively called me by name or ventured "How's it going?" Being a small-town boy, I knew enough not to actually tell them, but to say, "Oh, just barely gettin' by," to which they'd reply, "Well, that's about all you can expect," and I'd say, "Yup." So now I'm a local.

A friend once told me that I'm ahead of my time here, that is, I'm stuck in the sixties, but Lyons is stuck in the fifties.

I think all I had in mind at first was to get out of the hot, sticky, crowded Midwest and become the kind of guy who knew the names of the pools on a great trout stream, knew the hatches and fly patterns, knew where to find dry wood for a fire on a cold day and otherwise just felt at home. And if that stream wasn't 100 percent natural, then I'd know of some that were.

From that standpoint, I can say that my life has been an unqualified success. I guess I've gotten used to it all by now—even gotten blasé about some things—but, luckily, I still get knocked out by where I am on a pretty regular basis.

Sometimes it happens when I just walk out my front door at home to go look in the mailbox. There'll be traffic on the road out front, but there are some pretty foothills to the south and west that are a hell of a lot farther away than they look. I've lived here long enough to be able to calculate, or at least come to grips with, the distances. Even though I'm down in the mouth of a little valley here, I can see farther than I ever could in Illinois or Minnesota or Ohio.

I'm not too far from a good-sized town, but there are things that make me feel nicely removed: the hills, the eagles in the air and the fact that when I make the last turn west heading up to my house, the sandstone ridges do something to the public radio station I listen to that makes Vivaldi's *Four Seasons* sound like it was being played on kazoos.

And, not incidentally, there's a little creek across the road with some brown trout in it. These are not the most gorgeous hills or the most magnificent creek in the Rocky Mountains, but they are nonetheless *in the Rocky Mountains,* and if you were born a midwesterner you'll never outgrow the idea that this is exotic stuff.

Something like a sense of place kicked in when I moved here, and I realized that I felt genuinely comfortable for the first time in my life. The air was clear and dry enough; the rocks and trees were the right color; the water was as cold as I thought it should be. Maybe this was profound, or maybe it was just the result of watching too many western movies as a kid. Whatever, it has never worn off.

Not everything that's happened to me out here has been wonderful, but even when things were grim, the scenery was still gorgeous and the fishing was good. There was always the consolation that I was a boy from the Midwest who had infiltrated a new environment—creating only a few ripples in the process—and learned to be at home in the Rocky Mountains. So whatever unpleasant crap was happening to me, I knew it could have been worse—I mean, I could have been poor and troubled in Cleveland.

If I haven't become a genuine westerner, I at least now hold some of the appropriate opinions. I think my part of the country is being used as a nuclear waste dumping colony by the East, and if we were smart, all of us west of the Mississippi would secede.

And when a book reviewer refers to Tom McGuane as "a Marlboro man with a taste for quiche," I see it as typical Eastern Seaboard myopia, as if brilliant novels written by someone from the Rocky Mountains—or anywhere outside of New York City—somehow violate a law of nature.

Interestingly, many of the people I fish with now are also transplanted midwesterners, and I think we all get into this to some degree. After all, life is going to be the way it is no matter what, but we live in a place we like now and that means a lot to those of us who appreciate countryside.

Even after quite a few years of fishing the Family Pool, someone is bound to poke the fire during a lull in the conversation and say, as if he'd just noticed, "Shore is purty here, ain't it?"

Relatives back home tell me I speak like that now—with a western accent—although I can't hear it myself. To me it sounds perfectly normal.

5

GAR

SOMEWHERE IN THE MIND of every angler there is a mythical fish. For a trout fisherman it might be an Atlantic salmon on a fly rod—that whole sport of kings business. For a northern pike fisherman it might be a musky. Interestingly enough, for most bass fishermen it's just a bigger bass.

Some fishermen go nuts for salt water, and the mythical fish becomes the bonefish or, if they're into size, the tarpon. A.K. tried tarpon fishing for the first time two summers ago, with a friend in Florida. He sent me a postcard from the

Keys that I couldn't read. It looked like it had been written in a hurry on a moving boat. I could only make out a few odd words and phrases like, "rain and wind . . ."; "silver . . ."; "at least 90 pounds . . ."; "less than ten seconds . . ."; "thought I'd . . ." and "Jesus!"

When he got home I learned that he had hooked and lost one enormous fish in a week and that it was, as everyone claimed, amazing. He wanted me to go with him next time and I said I would, but when the next season came around he had mellowed and we never quite got around to it. There were too many good mayfly hatches going on; too many trout to catch closer to home.

I've seen fishermen lose it over tarpon, but for some reason it didn't take with A.K.

Whatever the mythical fish is, it has to get to you in a certain, indefinable way, and it's probably not something you're going to catch every day. Often it's something you may, for one reason or another, *never* catch. Maybe it's even better that way.

WHEN I first heard about longnose gar fishing, it just sounded like a weird and perhaps neat thing to try: so weird, in fact, that no one I know had ever done it, though some had heard stories. This is how quixotic sporting adventures usually begin to take shape.

It seems that in certain warm, slow-flowing creeks and rivers in the Mississippi drainage there lives a large, prehistoric fish called a longnose gar, one of five species of gar found in North America. Among the gars it is the thinnest with the longest nose or, more properly, "beak." Hence the name.

The fish has the body of a very long, skinny northern pike, and the snout looks a little like the bill of a swordfish, except that it opens and is filled with zillions of snarly teeth. Its overall color is a sort of nondescript grayish brown, darker on the back, with a few spots on the tail.

A longnose gar is also armored like a dinosaur. According to the official International Game Fish Association literature, the fish's bony, overlapping, diamond-shaped scales have been known to deflect arrows and even the occasional rifle bullet.

Supposedly the meat of the longnose gar is edible, although there are dissenting opinions on that, and you'll hear varying reports on how good it is, what its texture is like and what kind of people are willing to clean one. "Poor white trash eat 'em," I was once told, which means they're probably delicious. The fish's green eggs, however, are poisonous.

How could you call yourself a fisherman and not want to go try and catch one of these things, especially when you hear, in a roundabout way, that they can be taken on a fly rod?

So in the third week in May, Larry Pogreba and I headed off to go gar fishing. We'd been talking about trying this for a couple of seasons, although we'd never quite gotten around to it. But then Larry bought a bird dog from a breeder in southeastern Kansas and had to go pick him up. It so happened that the slow creeks and rivers in that part of the country are known to hold gar, and it was spring, when the gar fishing is supposed to be good. It seemed like the perfect excuse.

Larry also used to live in the area and still has many friends there—folk artists, catfish farmers, people who would know about such things—that he could call to see if the rivers were clear yet. Longnose gar spawn in May or June and are concentrated at these times, making them easier to locate. You want the water to be clear so the sight-feeding fish can see your lure. Naturally, the rains also come in those months, making clear water a gamble.

We went in Larry's 1979 Cadillac Brougham d'Elegance, the only appropriate vehicle to take gar fishing. When we heard that the streams were right, we filled the big trunk with belly boats, strapped a canoe on the roof for good measure and, because we didn't know what we'd be getting into, packed every item of heavyweight fly tackle we had.

I guess I can't really say we didn't know what to expect. Larry had somehow located a Federal Circuit Court judge in Arkansas City who is an expert at this. By all accounts, this guy is the Ernie Schwiebert of fly-fishing for longnose gar. Larry, who is never shy about this kind of thing, called the guy up. His Honor was a little vague over the phone, but it sounded as though if we showed up on his doorstep, he might take us fishing.

The judge also explained the basics of gar fishing with a fly rod—again, somewhat vaguely. The fish's beak is so thin and hard that a regulation fishhook will seldom sink and hold, so the few true afficionados fish for them with a length of frayed nylon rope. No hook at all, just rope. When the gar bites this, his teeth get tangled up in it and you can land him, although exactly why he bites it remains unexplained. We'd heard about this before, but it was good to be told by someone who had actually done it.

That is, you can land him *sometimes*. Even if the rope holds, it's said the fish puts up a horrendous fight and may well break your leader as he tailwalks and cartwheels down the river. And they're big, too. A 22 incher is only a year old and they grow quickly. The current world record (from Texas) is a 50 pounder. We saw a few that would have gone 4 feet—but I'm getting ahead of myself.

Word was the rivers and streams were clear, but the day we drove out it rained hard around Winfield and Ark City where we planned to fish—a couple of inches by most accounts. We heard about it on the radio and we could see it from as far off as Hays: the enormous, charcoal-colored sky down in the southeast corner of the horizon. We might have turned back if we hadn't had an expensive dog to pick up.

We stayed with a friend of Larry's in Wichita, ate some great, cheap Mexican food and spent our first evening listening to some very loud, very good jazz at a club called Seasons.

It rained hard again that night. At two in the morning I was riding shotgun in the Cadillac. The streets of Wichita were wet and glistening with reflected neon. I could still hear that great tenor sax, and I may have been a little drunk. I was disoriented until it occurred to me that this is how Russell Chatham would go gar fishing. Then I felt better.

The next morning Larry called a friend to ask how the rivers were. He listened, nodded, hung up and turned to me, quoting, "High and muddy as hell."

It didn't sound good, but these things always come down to the same conclusion: We drove 600 miles and now we're here. Might as well try it.

Now it seems that in Kansas, gar are not considered a game fish, officially or otherwise. In fact, the fishing regulations don't mention them at all, so one is left to assume that they come under the heading "other species," on which there are no bag limits or tackle restrictions. We'd gotten our first hint at the low esteem in which gar are held in Kansas when we bought our fishing licenses and some nylon rope in Hutchinson and told the guy what we were up to.

"Why?" he asked, honestly curious.

Not wanting to get into a big deal about the aesthetics of sport, Larry said, "We heard they were good to eat."

"Eat 'em all," the guy said, "no one'll care."

Clearly he didn't know much about gar fishing. He even sold us the wrong kind of rope. He gave us the hard kind you use to tie up boats. What you need is the *soft* kind.

Over the course of the next few days we learned that, although some local fishermen had caught gar accidentally— and then didn't know what to do with them—none we talked to had ever tried to do it on purpose with any kind of tackle, let alone a fly rod. They did sometimes shoot them, however, both for low-grade kicks and, supposedly, as a service to the environment.

Longnose gar, we were told, are not only big, ugly and inedible, they also eat up the bass, catfish, crappies and other respectable game fish, or at least compete with them for food.

Consequently, they should be exterminated. One can only wonder how the bass, catfish and etc. survived during those millions of years before there were farm boys with rifles to protect them from the gar.

Apparently some maniacs like to torture them, too. We learned that if you stick a longnose gar's snout in deep, thick mud he'll smother, and that if you prop his beak open with a stick and throw him back in the water he'll drown. During those conversations I found myself wishing, for the first time in my life, that there was an animal rights activist around. A real shrill, crazy one.

When we told people we wanted to catch longnose gar on fly rods, they either laughed, frowned or glanced suspiciously at our Colorado license plates, but these are mostly nice people (the few psychotics notwithstanding) and no one actually asked us to leave town.

Naturally, there's a good side to this. Hot bass and catfish holes are highly valued and closely guarded, but any stranger on the side of the road will happily direct you to the best gar water in the state, although he might not put it in those terms.

One guy, in a made-over garage bait shop, was also amused, but he did warm to the idea and offered a few suggestions which were thoughtful, though they turned out to be wrong. "I seen people catch gar," he said. "Looked like a hell of a lot of fun."

This guy sold, among other things, a brand of stink bait so potent that, it's said, all you have to do is pour some on the bank and collect the catfish as they crawl out of the water to get at it.

As we drove south in search of the judge, we stopped to look at the Walnut River and found a pod of gar rising under a bridge. Well, they weren't really "rising," although that's what it looked like to a couple of trout fishermen. We found out later that they were coming to the surface to fill what some call lungs and others call swim bladders. We knew these were gar because they were about 3 feet long and now and then we could see a long, toothy beak break the surface. I, for one, had never seen a gar before, but I knew they weren't alligators and gar was the only other possibility.

We fished there for a couple of hours with chunks of rope tied clumsily to heavy fly leaders. The water was brown and thick with the visibility right at zero. We didn't feel much hope and, sure enough, never got a strike.

That was just as well. We learned later that the hard nylon rope we were using would have slipped right through the teeth of a gar.

After asking around a little we did eventually find the judge (he was known locally as "Fumbling Frank" the gar fisherman), and, as we suspected, he likes gar more than most. The day we spent with him he told us lots of stories about them and there was admiration in his voice. He said he'd fished all over the world, in both fresh and salt water, and that he'd never caught anything that fought like a big longnose gar.

He said it was actually possible to painstakingly extricate the nylon rope from a gar's teeth and release it, but that he usually whacked them soundly behind the eyes with a blunt instrument and gave them to a family he knew who liked to eat them. He'd never tasted the meat himself—said he preferred bass and quail.

He also showed us how to rig gar flies, something you won't find in even an advanced fly-tying manual. It's pretty logical, really. You start with a standard bead and spinner setup, attach a split ring to the bottom of that and tie the frayed rope to the ring. The judge used a full-dress pattern: white rope with a topping of orange yarn.

Naturally, we'd been doing it all wrong. Larry and I have been fishing for a long time, but our imaginations had come up short at the concept of a fly with no hook.

The judge said we were in serious trouble because of the muddy water. He would never fish for gar under conditions like these, but since we were here, he thought maybe we could find a clear stream out in the rolling Flint Hills country 30 miles to the east.

I asked him when he thought the rivers might clear, and he didn't think it would be anytime soon. "Middle of next month, maybe," he said.

It made sense when you looked at the countryside. The creeks drain off of fairly flat, soft ground, and they are deep and slow. These are not the fast mountain streams we Rocky Mountain types are used to, and it's easy to see how the sediment would take weeks to either settle or flush out.

Larry followed in the Cadillac while the judge and I led the way in his old pickup. He drove a little too fast for the dirt roads, but it was a hot, muggy day and the moving air felt good. Larry hung back to keep out of the dust cloud.

I did my best to interrogate the judge about the fishing in the area, and it worked out well as soon as I realized that he didn't necessarily answer questions in the same order they were asked. I also learned the name of the owner of every spread we passed, how much stream and how many ponds he had, how the hunting there was and what breed of bird dog the guy preferred. We crossed many creeks on many one-lane bridges, and they were all dirty.

Muddy streams aside, this is really wonderful, quiet, rich country. Not much livestock, not many houses. The Flint Hills are low, rolling, rocky pastureland punctuated generously with slow creeks and thick hardwood groves. Others know more about this than I do, but it seemed like what you had along the creeks were the remnants of old-growth hardwood forests with enormous, mature trees and huge standing snags full of woodpecker holes. A couple of decades in the Rocky Mountains had made me rusty on the deciduous trees, but I could tell the oaks, maples, beeches, walnuts and a couple of others.

There are wild turkeys here, huge, fat white-tailed deer and lots of quail that the judge hunts with Brittany spaniels and a 28-gauge shotgun.

And, of course, fish: largemouth, smallmouth and spotted bass; channel and flathead catfish; white and black crappies; redear and green sunfish, bluegills, warmouth, rock bass, white bass, not to mention gar. And the streams have that limestone chemistry that is known to grow large fish quickly.

I'M told the summers in southeast Kansas are awful: blisteringly hot, oppressively humid, with clouds of biting bugs in the air, fleets of leeches in the water and chiggers. (Any of you who grew up in the Midwest will remember chiggers.) I believe it because even May was hotter and damper than I like, reminding me of childhood midwestern summers when I'd go for days feeling beaten by the heat and humidity and spend my nights lying awake, stark naked, sweating into a hot pillow, thinking about moving to the Rocky Mountains when I grew up.

I did just that, and in my first summer in Colorado I began to equate the clear, dry western air with a kind of intellectual clarity. Now, when I go east into the humidity, I feel fuzzy and hesitant, like my head was stuffed loosely with dubbing material.

It occurred to me that this was the year I'd weaseled out of going to the big family reunion in Illinois. I'd said I was too busy, and when that didn't wash I admitted to my sister that I just couldn't face the hot, sticky Midwest in high summer.

Southeast Kansas is a lot like the part of Illinois where I was born, and I found it strangely resonant. There were some things to remind me where I was, like the scissortail flycatchers, but the cardinals and eastern jays were just like the ones at home, and it got me to thinking.

Did you ever go through that phase where you just had to disengage from your family, no matter what? I did, and during that time I formulated this theory that childhood imprinting and family heritage either didn't matter or could be overcome through force of intellect, but now I'm not so sure about that.

I've noticed that at a certain age things begin to float to the surface. If you beat yourself up when you were younger, those old wounds start to throb at odd times, and you may now and then find yourself thinking and speaking in what can only be an ancestral voice, because it sure as hell isn't you, but it still had to come from somewhere.

Like it or not, I'm a midwestern English/German mutt; consequently, I'm quirky, moody, liberal, opinionated and have this nagging suspicion that things would be better in the long run if I and a few people like me ruled the world.

I guess there's just a kind of midwestern hybrid vigor that I recognize and understand. My girlfriend Susan, for instance, is a Norwegian/Spanish cross from Michigan, sort of a smouldering, sexy, Viking bullfighter. I've been told we're an interesting pair, but we do connect in some pretty fundamental ways. Before I left for Kansas she said she'd still love me whether I caught a gar or not, but if I did she wanted to help me eat it because her Norwegian side likes fish.

I ended up wondering if I'd have to explain at some point why I wouldn't go to Illinois to see the family, but I'd go to Kansas to try to catch some ugly fish that no one likes. I figured if it came to that I'd simply have to explain that it was a matter of sport. Dad and Uncle Leonard are dead now, but there are still some people in the family who would understand.

ANYWAY, the stream fishing there in southeast Kansas— when the streams were clear—would not only be good, but also uncrowded. Apparently the bass fishermen like the ponds and reservoirs, and these bodies of water are sometimes hard to get permission to fish. But no one seems to worry too much about the creeks. Most of them are private, but the judge said you can usually get on any of them just by asking. Of course, he was a local and a member of the judiciary to boot, so he might have a slightly unrealistic view of that.

The little stream the judge took us to was as muddy as all the others we'd seen, but we decided to fish it anyway because we were there, it was our best shot and because some enormous fish were boiling in a long, slow pool. I watched one near the bank that was clearly 4 feet long. "That's a good one," the judge agreed.

This gar would materialize out of the thick, muddy water in the spookiest way imaginable, hang there just on this side of visibility for the split second it took him to take a gulp of air and then vanish again. It was fascinatingly ugly, and the whole enterprise began to seem eerie and possibly dangerous.

I fished from the bank for a while, largely because I was afraid to get into the water with these things, but after Larry and the judge went out in their belly boats and weren't attacked right away, I decided to try it.

I'll spare you the blow-by-blow account and just say we never caught one. The water was muddy, so the gar couldn't see our flies, and as big and vicious as these fish looked, they seemed to be a little on the skittish side. After we'd made a few casts in the general direction of one, he'd just seem to disappear.

I did get pretty good looks at a couple of fish, and they *were* ugly, but they also had a kind of dim-witted, prehistoric charm. I could see how it would be possible to stand on the bank and shoot them with a rifle as they came to the surface, but I couldn't see why you'd want to do that. They were like manatees: big and unattractive enough to scare you at first, although they were basically just homely and harmless. It felt kind of hypnotic just to be floating around in the warm, muddy water with these big, shy things.

I did want to catch one, but I wasn't sure how eager I'd be to kill it. I probably would have, though, if only because I had a recipe for gar balls: gar meat mixed with rice and vegetables, rolled into hush puppy–sized balls and deep fried. Kansas soul food.

Larry and I did get a couple of halfhearted strikes, but the fish always came loose after making a single, dull thud on the end of the line. The judge finally explained the problem. We were instinctively setting the hook when we'd feel the tug of the fish, but of course that's wrong because there *is* no hook. When a gar takes your rope fly you're supposed to give him slack. The more he mouths the fly the better the chances his teeth will get tangled up in it. It would have helped to know that earlier, although smarter fishermen might have figured it out.

Late that afternoon the judge took us to a nearby pond where the water was clear to catch some bass, just so it wouldn't be a total loss. The pond was behind a low hill and one bank was already in shade. We fished from float tubes and caught big bass and respectable bluegills for several hours, using top-water bugs with hooks.

There were some fine, big fish in there, and it was so familiar and comforting I had even more fun than I normally would have. While the light was still good, I took several photos of fat bass lying on the tube of the belly boat with frog-painted #4 fly rod Hula Poppers in their jaws, the kind of pictures you've seen a thousand times, but go on taking anyway. I must have dozens of slides like that. The size of the bass changes, but otherwise they all look alike. It's been the same float tube for years, too, although going through those shots I can see how the orange patch on the front of the tube has faded to pale pink over the seasons.

Somewhere around dusk, something shifted and this became a normal bass-fishing trip that included a long, strange detour.

Before we went our separate ways, we shared a ceremonial beer and some jerky with the judge. He said he was sorry the gar fishing hadn't been better, and he said he liked adventurous fishermen like us who are willing to try something new.

He'd told me that he had one gar-fishing buddy, and I got the impression that a serious gar fisherman living in bass and catfish country might get a little lonely. Then he shook our hands, got in his pickup and drove away.

I asked Larry if he had any idea where we were.

"Yeah," he said, "sort of."

THE next day—armed with the proper flies—we tried the Walnut River again, from the canoe this time and in the company of a friend of Larry's who was at loose ends at the moment and thought this might be fun. This guy was a legitimate folk artist working in a medium I'd never heard of before: surrealist road-kill sculpture. Using parts from various dead animals killed by cars, he would assemble the carcasses of fictitious creatures that he would then leave on the side of the road to be found by innocent passersby. I couldn't help wondering what this guy would do with a gar if he caught one, and if he'd expect us to help.

But, although we gave it a good try and saw some fish boiling in the muddy water, we still couldn't connect. I got one light strike, set the hook without thinking, and then said to Larry, "Godammit." It was obvious we needed clear water in the streams and just as obvious we wouldn't get it anytime soon, so we picked up Larry's bird dog and headed back to Colorado.

WE were a couple of hours out on I-70 when it occurred to me that we might have caught some gar on minnows or, since we didn't have any and were a long way from a bait shop, worms. You know, the way any fisherman who isn't a raving purist approaches muddy water. I grew up in the Midwest, after all, and I do think I remember where to find bait along a creek. That wouldn't have been dependable, either, but it's how the locals catch them by accident, and we could have tried it.

I wasn't exactly sorry we hadn't done that—when you set out to catch something on a fly rod, then that's how you want to do it—but, as I said, it occurred to me.

In the final analysis, I guess it's possible that too much attention to sport can isolate you from reality. Clearly gar fishing is not trouting, and I wondered if we were being snots by not fishing bait or, for that matter, not bringing rifles.

One of the things I like about Larry is that he addresses things as they are. I can't say what he'd have done on his own, but I know he'd have come back with some fish. Not that I cramped his style. Larry probably thought, Okay, I'm out with a fly-fishing snob, so that's how it's going to be. If we can't catch them the way they're caught, we'll fail to catch them in high style, but we won't do it halfway.

It's like something he once said about movies. "You want four stars, or none," he said, *"Citizen Kane* or *Nymphoid Barbarians in Dinosaur Hell."* We've never talked about it, but I think he feels the same way about fishing. It should either be high sport or deep funk.

Rather than stew about it, I started to get to know Dutch, Larry's new, handsome little German shorthair pointer, who was crouched nervously in a corner of the big backseat. Dutch wasn't in the best of moods, never having ridden in a car before and not knowing who the hell we were or where we were taking him, but he eventually decided I was okay.

6

POCKET
WATER

ONE AFTERNOON LAST SUMMER I went fishing for the first
time with Ken Arnold, a friend from Philadelphia.
Ken is a publisher and, although he's a young man, he still
manages to be of the old school. That is, he operates in
what's euphemistically called the "real world," but he also
sometimes prints a book for no other reason than that it's a
good one. I like him.

Ken was in the area on business and he was pressed for
time, as publishers always seem to be, but he'd managed to

break loose for most of a Saturday and, as luck would have it, he'd thought to pack some comfortable clothes and a rod. He said that, however busy he was, he didn't want to leave Colorado without wetting a fly line, even if it was only for a few hours.

It was a summer weekend, which meant a lot of the easy to get to places would be crowded, and we didn't have time for a full-bore safari to some fabulous spot. I wanted this to be as good as possible, and my guess was that Ken would appreciate a little peace and quiet, so I decided to take him to a small pocket water stream not far from here that makes for a quick but easygoing half-day trip.

Since it's best to start visiting fishermen off with realistic expectations, I carefully warned him that we'd see some pretty country and have some interesting fishing for wild, though not actually native, trout, but that the fish themselves probably wouldn't be enormous.

"That sounds fine," Ken said, and I hoped it would be. You can describe the probable quality of the fishing as accurately as possible, and you can even explain that, although you write about fishing for a living, you are a reporter rather than an expert, but I've found that when you take someone out, there's no way to remain completely blameless.

THE pocket water streams I know are all here in the Rocky Mountains—it's the severe gradient of rough country that gives them that tumbling, broken character—and most are small enough that all you'll ever need to get around in them is hippers, or "ditch boots" as they're called hereabouts. Most are known not so much for themselves as for being this or that fork of a larger creek or river.

These pocket waters usually fit the standard small-stream profile pretty well. For one thing, they're not famous, and few, if any, fly shops or Trout Unlimited chapters are named for them. They're probably not widely known outside their own neighborhoods, and even then there's usually a river or a set of lakes nearby where the fishing is thought to be better.

The best ones don't have roads running along them—at least not good, passenger-car roads—but just wander out of wilderness areas or national parks. Where they flow under a county road at an old Civilian Conservation Corps bridge, there will be a turnout or maybe even a campground. A mile in either direction from the bridge the thing will have been fished, and may actually have been pretty well fished out, a fact that will give it the local reputation of being a so-so little trout stream at best.

As I said, the local T.U. chapter probably won't be named after this creek, but you can bet there are a handful of guys in that club who fish it often and know it well. After a little casual exploring one season, they discovered it was quite good—surprisingly good, actually, considering its size and reputation—so now they think of it as *their* stream, and knowing the thing is right there on the map for anyone to see sometimes makes them a little bit nervous. Having found all this out more or less on their own makes them feel cagey, so they may not talk about it much except among themselves, and if they do, they won't use its name. (Now that I think about it, that's what I did with Ken. I told him we'd be fishing "a little creek I know about.")

Then, after a summer or two of exploration and discovery, one of these guys said something like, "You know, I think I had more fun this year on little Such-and-such Creek than I did on the Platte and the Henry's Fork put together." The others thought about it for a minute and nodded. "Yeah, all things considered, you're probably right."

That was a few years ago. They still say that every winter, but they no longer seem surprised, and now they may let a year slip by when they don't even *go* to the Henry's Fork.

You usually start out on a little pocket water stream simply because it's close to home and does have some trout in it, but it can sneak up on you until it begins to define you as one of those curious, secretive types who shy away from famous rivers with crowds and hatch charts and fishermen's access signs along the highway. You want to work out for yourself how and where to get on the water, and you don't really want to know what hatch to expect or the exact date it's likely to begin. You come to see that the more you know about things like that, the less likely you are to have a real adventure.

POCKET water is just what it sounds like: It's steep, fast, broken, braided, loud, jumbled with boulders and deadfalls, pocked with deep holes, scoured by short, fast riffles and plunge pools, punctuated with eddies and backwaters, and generally filled with large and small pockets where the trout hide.

As scenery, pocket water is usually gorgeous in a rugged, hidden sort of way. Around here the surrounding slopes will be dry and rocky, forested in pine, spruce and/or fir with patches of aspen, but down near the stream it will be moist and lush with moss-covered rocks, ferns, bigtooth maples, willows, dogwoods, water birches and a whole guidebook full of wildflowers.

Year after year the fallen pine needles, aspen leaves and other organic junk washes down the slopes with the melting snow to join the leaves and stalks already there. Some of this falls into the stream to become insect food, while the rest composts into a rich, black, boggy soil that's held by mats of roots, but that still springs a little under your feet.

If it was flatter and there was more of it, it would seem dense and eastern, but it's too narrow and you can see out of it too easily. As it is, it's one of the richest, greenest, coolest places you'll find in summer, and the coldest in winter, with the deepest snow.

The falling currents are loud enough, and there are so many of them talking at once, that eventually you'll begin to hear voices speaking single words clearly. The stream will say, "Hey," or "Whoa," or maybe, "Oops." A.K. has mentioned this, too, so it's not just me.

· · ·

Many of the fly fishermen I know avoid pocket water because it's difficult—not in the high sport, spring creek sense of snooty fish, tiny bugs and long, artful drifts, but sort of a close-range difficult where, if you're doing it right, you don't look especially graceful. There are so many conflicting currents and obstructions that long, luxurious, dry fly drifts are impossible and there's usually so much brush that back casts snag on every other try. You'll do some crawling and climbing. It's possible that you'll get your hands dirty.

Good pocket water fishers work in close on the theory that the less line you have lying on the water, the better your drift will be and the more control you'll have. The epitome of this is dapping, where nothing but the fly—suspended under the tip of the rod on a few feet of leader—touches the water. In practice, you may have a few inches to a few feet of leader on the surface, but the procedure is about the same: Get as close as you can, make a short, flicking cast and follow the drift with the rod tip.

As a rule, I'll fish a short, downstream drift when at all possible because it gives me more control and, if I want to put some action on the fly, it will be moving in the right direction. It was Leonard Wright who pointed out that a bug struggling in the current always struggles *up*stream, against the flow. This is a man who's spent days at a time lying on his belly on the bank of a trout stream watching insects, so I figure I can take his word for it.

Then again, so many situations present themselves in pocket water that it's helpful to have a fairly large repertoire of hook, S-curve, snake, reach, pile and other creative slack line casts to choose from, no two of which will be quite alike. This is not the kind of thing you can practice on a casting pool, you have to go out and make your mistakes on site.

Naturally, there are some tackle adjustments. That is, any old rod and line will do, but if a fly fisher doesn't have to fine-tune his gear a little bit, he feels cheated. I like to use a size heavier line than the rod I'm using calls for, because the extra weight loads the rod better on shorter casts. This is a little like screwing in the cylinder bore choke tube because the ducks will be at close range. And that heavier line should have a good dry fly leader attached because you'll often be casting more leader than line, so how that leader works will make a big difference.

I tie my leaders based on a formula A.K. developed back in Michigan. He scribbled it down for me years ago on a piece of blue notebook paper and slipped it to me folded. I felt as though I should commit it to memory and then eat it.

Without going into detail, these things have a slow, gradual taper at the butt, a fast taper a little forward of the middle and then a long tippet. The fat part is tied from sections of stiff, almost wiry monofilament, and the thin part is made of the loosest, limpest leader material you can find.

A.K. has a whole lecture on leaders, having to do with how the energy flowing down the line wants to dissipate due to the resistance of the air, so you maintain it by feeding it first through stiff material, then through a steep taper, and finally into the flimsy stuff at the end that turns over nicely, but still molds itself to the shapes in the current.

And all this directed by the hundreds of muscles in your arm and hand through a fine old favorite fly rod, the precise wiggle of which you have encoded on your subconscious so that, when you're hot, at least, you picture the spot where the fly should be and it appears there as if by remote control.

A.K. isn't kidding about any of this. You could say he's a stickler for detail. I've even seen him take out a pocketknife and shave the cork grip on an expensive bamboo rod because he didn't quite like the way it fit the heel of his casting hand. I winced aloud at that, and he said, "What the hell. If you can't use the thing, what good is it?"

Most fly fishers like to use short rods for pocket water, say, around 7 feet, while those who do a lot of dapping want the longest stick they can feed through the brush. Anglers like me who are always afraid they'll inadvertently shortchange themselves if they get too specialized tend to split the difference at around 8 feet. A good pocket water rod has to be able to do a lot of different things well, so it shouldn't be either too short or too long, too light or too heavy.

Mike Clark, my favorite bamboo rod maker, is currently building me a 7-foot-9-inch, quick-action (but not *too* quick) 5-weight designed especially for small-stream fishing. We talked this over for quite a while, referring to some other rods we've cast in terms of action, and came up with something resembling a Garrison taper, to which Mike has added some of his own refinements.

Then we moved on to the cosmetics, where we got a little carried away. The rod will be a two-piece with a slightly flared butt, traditional cigar grip and mortised cap and ring seat with a walnut spacer. It will have full antique-style intermediate wraps in brown and gold, and the ferrules and reel seat will be blued and engraved.

The blued hardware cuts down on ferrule flash, which some say is important when fishing in close quarters, but there's no excuse for the engraving. It's just neat.

I got so excited about the rod that I ordered a Peerless #2 reel to go on it. If you've never seen a Peerless, it looks like an old Bogdan with black side plates and a silver serpentine crank with a counterweight.

Things like this are tricks, or, if you prefer, meditation aids. I'll be out there on a stretch of pocket water, hunkered down behind a rock, casting to a run one and a half rod lengths away, and I'll be holding in my right hand the baby-smooth cork grip of an expensive bamboo rod that was custom made for just this. The fly will appear at the precisely correct spot in the current as if by the will of God.

And if not, then at least my friend will continue to make a living selling hand-planed bamboo rods to middle-aged mystics.

. . .

I GUESS I particularly enjoy the sneaky aspects of this kind of fishing. I like staying low, wading quietly, hiding behind boulders, paying attention to what's behind me—not only to keep from fouling my back cast but also to keep my silhouette screened by trees—and trying to keep in the shade so I don't stand out too much. Once you're in the right head, this all becomes second nature, so you don't have to keep thinking about it. The broken water itself also acts as cover, and it's surprising how close you can get to a trout without spooking him.

This kind of thing makes me feel like I'm really in the water with the fish. When I can sneak to within a rod's length of a trout and catch him, I feel like I've executed a pure, catlike animal maneuver, which more than makes up for the fact that the cast was probably less than elegant.

And in many cases I can also congratulate myself on knowing that fish was there in the first place, because reading pocket water can be tricky. Sure, trout still like to lie in relatively calm spots next to or below faster, food-carrying currents, but the more broken the water is, the better those holding spots are hidden.

I like to think in terms of scale. How big a lie does, say, a foot-long trout need? Not very. Smaller than a shoe box, smaller than a football, maybe about the size of an adult human footprint. With that in mind, even the roughest stretch of water opens up into a field of possibilities.

I usually approach a pocket water stream in one of two ways. Some days I'll cruise up it looking for more or less obvious holding spots: a slick behind a rock, a little plunge, a backwater, undercut, half-sunken log—the kind of thing anyone would pick out. This is a good way to make time and cover a good, long stretch of stream. Some days that's what I want out of it: the long, scenic stroll during which some fish are caught. Around dusk—or after dark on a moonlit night— I'll get up in the trees and hike quickly back to the truck. Sometimes I find I haven't gone nearly as far as I thought.

On especially good days it's possible to stay too long and

get caught out after sunset, but even in the dark, if you follow the sound of the stream, you can't possibly get lost, although you *can* walk into a tree. With this in mind, you disjoint the rod and carry it pointing behind you.

The stream will have been talking all day, but sometimes at dark it will begin to mumble in complete sentences: nothing profound, which has always been a disappointment to me, just things like, "Don't worry so much—and call your mother once in a while."

At other times I'll get very surgical about it, running at least a drift or two through everything that isn't white water. This is slower going, but it's usually more educational. On a good day I'll invariably take a couple of trout from absolutely inexplicable spots and walk away thinking, What the hell was he doing *there*? That sort of thing builds up in your subconscious so that, although you can't explain the mechanics of it, you can look at a stretch of water and get these suspicions about spots you would once have passed by.

And, of course, I'll always fish the big, magnificent pools you'll find here and there on most pocket water streams—the ones that allow for some real line-in-the-air fly casting. In fact, I've come to use them as indicators of fishing pressure.

The big pools are so obviously fishy looking that no one overlooks them, and they respond well to serious food-getting techniques employing things like worms and salmon eggs. On a heavily fished stretch of stream, you'll probably find that the pools hold no trout, or only a couple of small ones. But when I get to a place where the big pools give up decent-sized trout, I know I've walked far enough from the nearest easy access point that things are starting to get interesting.

THE little stream Ken and I fished that day is typical of pocket water in many ways. It's small, rough, pretty, and many fishermen who have lived in the county for ten years have never gotten around to fishing it farther than a twenty-minute walk from the turnoff. Near the campground it isn't especially good (and that works as excellent camouflage), but there are still miles of it up in the national forest and the wilderness area beyond that seem to be largely undisturbed, or at least disturbed so little it hasn't made a difference.

This particular stream may be a little bit unusual, because in a stretch of not much more than 10 miles you go from browns and rainbows to brook trout to cutthroats. It's hard to take the grand slam in a single day because this is a gradual, drawn-out transition, except for one place where a waterfall marks the spot above which you will never catch a brown trout.

The stream is no longer stocked where I fish it and, although most are there because of earlier plantings, the trout are now homegrown and self-sustaining; left, mostly forgotten and doing very well on their own, thank you. As I told Ken, they're wild, if not entirely native, and they look it. They're bright, strong and healthy—even the little ones.

I wasn't setting Ken up when I told him the fish wouldn't be big, because for the most part they're not. I fish this particular stream often and it's not unusual for me to work most of a day for two or three fish that might go 10 or 11 inches.

I have carefully adjusted my thinking over the years to make that all right, because I know too much horniness for big trout can ruin a fisherman, making him feel he's too good to fish just any old creek. Getting my head straight about this wasn't that hard, since I guess I've always preferred the company of people who *will* fish just any old creek.

Of course, having said that, I have to admit that the big-fish thing never entirely goes away. From time to time, in the more remote parts of this stream, I've taken several 15- and 16-inch trout, which I consider to be honest pigs in small water like that. A fisheries biologist told me I'd probably taken some of the biggest fish in that creek. I don't care who you are, you can't ask for any more than that.

The same man also told me I could righteously keep a fish

of that size from this stream ("anything over 14 inches" is what he said) because it was big and old and probably wouldn't winter over anyway.

That's probably true, but I still don't have the heart for it. When I take a couple of fish to eat they're usually 9-inch brookies. I put the big ones back out of sentiment and—let's be honest—because if they *do* happen to winter over and get even bigger the next summer, I know where they live.

OR maybe I just think I know. Sitting here at the desk, I can visualize some places where I've caught big trout, but when I try to remember exactly how to get to them, the picture gets a little fuzzy. With A.K., Ed and/or Mike Price, I've fished the whole stream from the county road bridge to the headwater lake and on up the feeder above that until it got too small to keep a trout wet. There's a lot of water in there, a lot to remember.

Still, I think I can walk right to the hole where I caught my first big cutthroats. A.K. and I had hiked up to a stretch we'd never fished before, and it was a pretty good walk. When we got back to the pickup that evening, we got out the map and figured we'd gone no less than 15 miles round-trip.

Anyway, we'd split up at a spot where we'd been getting some nice brook trout. A.K. wanted to work the water hard, see what was there and maybe keep a brace of 10 inchers for supper. I was anxious about what was on upstream. We were past the waterfall where the browns stop, way past the last rainbows, into the brookie water where you'd occasionally hang a small cutt.

The pool was a typical good spot: a deep, straight run with a plunge at the head and an almost glassy current down its middle. I was making time, eager to see what the water upstream looked like, but it was such a deep, fine-looking slot that I slowed down and fished it methodically.

After working the shallow tail and taking one small brookie, I cast the dry fly toward the back end of the deeper water and hooked a heavy fish. It turned out to be an honest 15-inch cutthroat with big spots and lots of reddish orange on it. This was in August, but the spawning colors hadn't faded yet. After all, at that altitude spring is in July.

I thought about killing the fish—to eat, of course, but also to show it to A.K. I knew he'd have two on a stringer the next time I saw him, and it would be fun to have a bigger one. I thought about it hard for thirty seconds, holding the trout in the water with his face into the current, and when he wiggled enough to show he was okay, I just let him go. General principle: when in doubt, release.

Then I dried the fly with a few false casts, flipped it 2 feet farther up in the run and hooked a cut that was the twin of the first one, only an inch longer and a little deeper in the belly. I thought, Okay, is *this* the one I'm supposed to show A.K. or is it a reward for turning the first one loose? I put the second fish back, too. Another general principle: when karmic implications are unclear, release.

MIKE Price and I made it to the headwater lake in September. We drove a dirt road to the wilderness area boundary and then hiked past miles of good water. That wasn't easy, but it was getting late in the year and we wanted to get to the lake so we could say we'd fished the whole thing.

On the way back out that night there was some car trouble. We were in Mike's 1952 military jeep, the one in original olive drab with the white star on the hood, into which Mike had put a Dodge V-8 engine. It's still not completely clear what's wrong with this thing, but there's a good chance the radiator can't handle the big motor. Anyway, it overheats.

We ended up stalled after dark in the middle of the dirt track 5 miles from the main road, with steam rising from the hood into the chilly air. It was just a matter of letting the thing cool down, and we'd had a good day, so if the trip home had to happen in 5-mile increments, then that's how we'd do it. Worse things have happened to both of us.

It was calm and quiet down there in the trees, even though
a snowstorm was blowing in and it had been cold and breezy
up high. Normally there'd be a dozen night sounds, identi-
fiable and otherwise, but all we could make out was the
hissing of the radiator.

That storm was why we'd gone in the first place. A good
snow wouldn't put the fishing off for the season, but it could
close the four-wheel-drive road until the following summer,
and we didn't want to end up wondering about that lake for
another nine months.

It had been perfect. We'd hiked in to the lake, fished
around it and gone on up the inlet creek to the last stretch of
trout water. We'd caught lots of fish, all cutthroats, and we
got several 16 inchers about as far up in there as you could
get and still expect to catch anything at all. There was no
trail, no sign of other fishermen, except for a single, ancient
salmon egg jar, and the fish were almost heartbreakingly easy
to catch.

As we stood there next to the spitting, steaming jeep, Mike
asked me if I was going to tell A.K. about this, the implica-
tion being that maybe I wouldn't. When I said yes, he said,
"Do you think he'll believe it?"

A.K. did believe it, but at the time I had to wonder. It was
just the kind of perfect story a writer would make up.

THIS is the kind of nearby stream that you can get casual
about and learn in your own good time. One day Ed and I
waded a couple of miles of it with binoculars and identified
nineteen species of birds. We sat for half an hour watching
a flycatcher nip mayflies out of the air and feed them to her
two chicks. The nest was in the root ball of a huge fallen
spruce tree. It was so well hidden that once the adult left and
the pink mouths of the chicks disappeared, it would just
vanish, even though you were looking right at it.

The flies were big Red Quills and there were some trout
rising. We were only a little sorry we didn't have rods. The

gear wasn't even back in the car. We knew we'd have to leave the fishing stuff at home if we were going to put in an honest afternoon of bird-watching.

And then just last summer, while going through a wild-flower book, I discovered that the purple flower along this stream we call monkshood is the same thing they call wolfs-bane in Europe. If you're a fan of old Lon Chaney, Jr., movies, you'll understand the gravity of that.

I DIDN'T tell Ken any of this. I just said there was a lot of water to fish and, pointing vaguely west, that high up there were some cutthroats, although that was too far for us to go in just an afternoon.

Maybe it was the normal paranoia that keeps you from revealing too much, even to a guy from out of town, or maybe it was because, although some great things have happened on this stream, I still see it as ordinary. I can drive to it in forty-five minutes, no place on it is more than a half day from home—given a four-wheel-drive vehicle to give you a head start—and from early July to sometime in September, it's always good.

But it's not so good that you don't dare show it to a friend. If Ken talked about it when he got home, he'd have said it was a gorgeous stream with okay fishing for pan-sized trout. Fun, but probably not worth a long trip.

I guess I love this stream for the same reason I like to hunt snowshoe hares more than deer. Bunnies, like the trout in this creek, are numerous, not too big, and they don't have antlers, so you don't get distracted by the idea of a trophy. Sure, there may be an old, hook-jawed, half-blind, nocturnal torpedo living in some dark undercut—if only because fishing mythology requires it—but that's not something you can count on.

And there's a nice feeling of constancy about it, too. I discovered the stream about twenty years ago when I was working as a garbageman. I've changed some since then, but the stream hasn't.

I ALMOST always use dry flies on this creek. They're fun, they're classy and trout living in pocket water have that aggressive, opportunistic streak that makes them snap at just about any odd bug floating by. It's a survival skill. If a pocket water trout wants to make it, he can't afford to be too shy or too careful. Most of the trout, big or small, work the open water in daylight where you can get at them.

This is also an unregulated, freestone stream, so it has fewer individual insects than a tailwater, but a much larger diversity of species. The fish see all kinds of odd bugs and they seem to keep open minds about food. This is the kind of water where you could do some business with a spider or a big bivisible pattern.

Like almost everyone else in the Mountain West, my favorite fast-water fly is the good old Royal Wulff in size 12 or 14. It's buoyant, easy to see and the fish seem to like it well enough most days. Other highly visible white-winged dry flies are also good and, yes, there are times when a hatch is on and the fish get a little bit picky, though usually this has more to do with size than with pattern.

There have been days here when I'd have been skunked if I hadn't had—at one time or another—Blue-winged Olives, Pale Morning Duns, Sulphers, Red Quills, Elk Hair Caddis flies and even Green Drakes, but that's actually pretty rare. It's just as likely that a hatch of #18 Blue-winged Olives means I have to switch from a size 12 Wulff to a #16.

A.K., being a professional fly tier and accuracy freak, has talked about tying pocket water versions of the common mayflies with standard bodies, a few extra turns of hackle and white wings for visibility. It's a tempting idea, like the special pocket water fly rod: the kind of thing that might not make a big difference, but that will make you feel *so* cool.

Mike Price, on the other hand, continues to fish the stream as he has all his life, that is, with a size 12 fan-wing Royal Coachman.

There are some good, heavy hatches on this stream from time to time, but I think I actually do better on pocket water when nothing much is happening in the insect department. The trout, always hungry and curious, seem a little more likely to inspect the single fly on the water. I've had some glorious days of dry fly fishing during which I never saw a rise that wasn't to my fly.

I've always liked water where the supposed science of fly selection doesn't apply. In places like this you're not after accuracy, but something more poetic and intuitive. Based on experience, tradition and maybe even myth, you guess where the fish will be, and you deliver this red, green, brown and white thing called a Royal Wulff that you can see and that you assume they'll bite. This is known as "pounding up" fish. It probably shouldn't work, but it does.

Sport is full of things like that. For instance, I've been told that if a goose hunter stands out in the open among his decoys and waves two black flags in the air, the geese will come in. And these are the same birds that will flare wildly when you raise a shotgun to your shoulder or even turn your head too quickly.

There's an explanation, as there always is: Geese on the ground flap their wings from time to time, either to stretch, dislodge parasites or—as the theory at hand goes—to signal their colleagues to come have some field corn.

A man waving black flags at geese is like tying white wings on a fly that doesn't really look like a bug anyway and then fishing it where no trout are feeding. It seems somewhat logical until you do it yourself, at which point it looks and feels stupid. But then, at least sometimes, it works. Fish bite, geese drop confidently out of the sky, and you think, This is weird, but great.

Good pocket water also tends to get me wondering. I'll see an especially difficult spot and begin to think, I can't make a

good cast to that. Okay, but if I can't, then neither can most
other fishermen, and the real hotshots don't fish here. This
could mean that a trout living there may have gone unmo-
lested for, who knows? Months? Years?

So I'll try it on the premise that a flubbed drift or a lost fly
isn't the end of the world. After all, no one is watching. Even
if I'm with someone, they're probably around a bend, and
there are many bends in water like this. I've taken some
rather nice trout this way, and lost a number of others.
Missing a fish isn't the end of the world, either.

While Ken was out of sight downstream that day, I tried
a cast like that. The spot was along the far bank: a tight little
back eddy in dark shade on the edge of a deep hole behind a
rock. A gnarled bigtooth willow hung out over the water,
moss was all over the bankside rocks and there was a patch
of bright blue chimingbells hanging in a patch of sunlight. I
thought, If a big fish doesn't live here, the world has gone
wrong.

My first couple of casts were short and the fly ripped past
out in the fast current. That was okay. It was a terrible drift,
but the fish—if one was there—wouldn't have seen it.

When I finally got it into the slick, the fly danced there for
a few seconds, and I could see a large shape come up under
it. The trout didn't take, but he was interested. When he
turned, I saw a 15-inch-long orange stripe, which would
make it a brook trout at least as long as that orange flash,
probably longer.

In fast water, a trout is never more than half seen in the
instant when he pulls his fish shape together out of all that
movement and then dissolves again. It can all be in your
mind, but when you see the flash of color, it's real.

I tried the same cast a dozen more times with two different
fly patterns, but I never saw the fish again. He was too big
and smart to be fooled twice. I marked the spot, figuring to
come back later after the fish had forgotten about all this.

. . .

As I said, Ken and I had wandered apart. Sometimes when I go out with a visiting fisherman I kind of shadow him, prepared to offer advice or a fly pattern, not as a guide but just as a good host. But I had gotten the feeling right off that Ken knew what he was doing and could probably stand to be left alone to explore. When we got on the water I'd gone into some kind of introductory spiel, but Ken had paid just enough attention to keep from being rude. He was squinting at the stream, picking out little creases and slicks that looked good, and tying on some kind of big fly with white wings.

I'd seen him a few times in the next couple of hours as we leapfrogged each other upstream, but we were always at some distance and the current was always too loud for much conversation. I knew he was catching fish, because he'd wave and grin. The guy who *isn't* catching fish shrugs.

When we finally met to discuss heading out—there was something on the schedule that meant he had to be back in Denver that evening—Ken told me about his best fish. Seems he'd hooked a pretty heavy brown trout at the head of a plunge pool and the fish had run downstream under some deadfall spruce trees. Ken had managed to get himself and his rod under the trees—tearing his waders and knocking his hat off in the process—but by the time he got out on the far side, the trout had broken off.

"I think it was a pretty big fish," he said.

He was delighted, which, in my humble opinion, places him in the highest order of fly fishermen: the guy who can tear up his gear, get wet, lose the fish and call it the best trout of the day.

"This is a real nice little stream," Ken said. I was afraid he was going to ask the name of it, but he didn't.

We headed back downstream toward the truck then, and I figured that when I came to the spot with the big brook trout in it I'd stop and try a few casts if there was time. I guess I wanted to show off a little: catch a big, pretty brookie in front of an audience, just like I knew what I was doing.

But from higher up on the bank it all looked different. At some point I knew we'd passed the spot, but I hadn't recognized it.

7

THE
HOG
HOLE

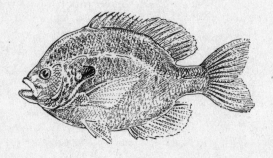

THERE ARE CERTAIN TEMPTATIONS a fisherman should approach gingerly, and these include the hog-hole mob scenes. We all know what a hog hole is, though some use other names for it: It's a piece of water—often, but not always, a tailwater fishery—that's filled with big, wild trout. The local wildlife agency probably describes it in florid terms—"a jewel in the crown of the state's fisheries," or

something like that. It's also public, easily accessible and
every fisherman in a three- or four-state area knows about it.

The South Park area of Colorado fits that description, and
that's why I hadn't fished it much in recent years.

This is a geologic park, not a state or national one: a high,
flat bowl of terrain that's surrounded on all sides by mountains. From one vantage point or another in South Park you
can see the Front Range, the Tenmile, Mosquito and Sawatch ranges, the Sangre de Cristos and the Wet Mountains.
Down in the bottom it's rolling, mostly treeless and covered
with scrubby prairie grasses that somehow seem to stay
brown all year long. The coniferous forests start at the edges
where the slopes begin to rise.

Like so many places in the West, its scale is deceptive. It
seems enormous when you first come over a ridge and see
these plains stretching away like Nebraska, then it begins to
feel smaller because you can see so much of it, then enormous again when you realize how long it takes to drive across
it. At night the headlights of an approaching car can just float
out there in the darkness like a planet.

Reports of early explorers had it covered with herds of
bison and antelope that were stalked by wolves and mountain
lions. Now there are a few cattle and occasionally some elk.
In the days when South Park held buffalo, the elk lived down
on the flatlands where the towns are now.

To hydrologists from those towns, the shallow depressions
on the course of the South Platte River through here con-
stituted neat, nearly ready-made impoundments, and so you
have Spinney Mountain and Eleven Mile reservoirs, and,
higher up, Antero.

South Park is well known for its strange, usually inclement
weather. Cold air will sometimes sink in there and, with
nowhere else to go, just sit like in a freezer chest. A cap of
clouds will often hang above the park when the rest of the
state is sunny. In warm weather the inevitable updrafts will
brew thunderstorms that seem to rattle around in the bowl,
bouncing off the mountain ranges. As for the wind, it blows

just about every day, starting in midmorning. Only the ve-
locity varies. Boats have been lost on the reservoirs in sudden
storms.

You can get soaked, frozen, windblown, drowned and/or
struck by lightning here, and on clear days, what with the
high altitude and thin atmosphere, you'll probably get sun-
burned. It's glorious: the western high plains at their best,
also the kind of thing that once scared most fishermen away.

THIS really is a great place for fish. The two lower reservoirs both have big trout and big northern pike, and the
stretches of the South Platte River above them have resident
trout as well as some good spawning runs in the spring and
fall. But this is all widely known, so the place is often
crowded.

Fishermen arrive predictably for the spawning runs, and
also when the ice goes off of Spinney Mountain and big
trout—rainbows, cutthroats and browns—wallow around in
the shallows. At least they're in the shallows until the pha-
lanxes of wading fishermen drive them out to deeper water.
Then, after what is sometimes a long wait for your chance at
the one ramp, you fish for them from a boat.

On weekends when the fishing is in full swing, the place
can look like Dunkirk; during the week it may only be
packed, although on odd weekdays that are impossible to
predict, you'll have more water than you can fish all to yourself.

Or at least that's what I'd heard. As I said, I hadn't fished
it for a while—not since it had caught on. The last time A.K.
and I tried Spinney it was a cold week in September. We
caught some 5-pound brown trout from belly boats in the
weedy channels at the inlet. There were three or four boats
on the water and a few wading fishermen. Relatively few.
This is a huge lake that can visually swallow up a lot of
people.

. . .

Of course, people do still catch fish here, sometimes even people who seem to have no idea what the hell they're doing. You'll now and then see photos in the newspapers of these guys holding enormous trout. They (the fishermen) often look happy but incredulous. There are so many fish—now protected by various regulations—that your odds of scoring are at least fair, even if you'll never know exactly how you did it. I've felt that way once or twice myself, and the people who do seem to know what they're doing all tell a different story.

South Park gets a good deal of ink in the newspapers, and we outdoor columnists counter charges of hot-spotting by saying that everyone already knows about it anyway. By now, that's true. Even the official Division of Wildlife fishing report admits that South Park is out of the bag and suggests that anglers who "cherish their solitude" avoid Spinney Mountain and that there *are* other good rivers besides the South Platte.

That last comment seems to be aimed, at least in part, at those who fish the stretch of the Platte River between Spinney and Eleven Mile, which is another traditional hog hole. Some years ago it reached the point where trout were being slaughtered in almost commercial proportions, so now the whole section—a little over 3 miles—has been designated Gold Medal Water by the Division of Wildlife, fishing is restricted to flies and lures only and it's all catch and release.

The river is no less crowded now than before the new regulations, although now the fishermen mostly use fly rods and fish from the standing position. The prediction of one fisheries manager has come true: When the no-kill rule was about to go on, he said, "There will be just as many fishermen, but less lawn furniture."

There's one notable exception to the catch-and-release rule. From the County Road 59 bridge downstream to the buoy line at Eleven Mile Reservoir (a mile and three-quarters of river) holders of a Trophy Trout Permit can keep one fish. This is a Division of Wildlife experiment. They're looking into the idea of marketing the single large trout the same way they do a big game animal. The original plan was to limit the harvest to trout 24 inches long or better, but when the permits were finally issued, they were good for "one fish," period.

Most of the permit holders are looking to bag one of the big spawning rainbows that come up out of Eleven Mile sometime in late winter or early spring. By most accounts, there really are some enormous trout in this run that are often described as being "in the 10-pound class." Although everyone knows this phrase commonly refers to any trout larger than about 4 pounds, it still has a certain ring to it.

Fishermen around here seem to be split on this issue. Some are openly eager to catch and kill one of the big spawners, presumably to mount. Many, though not all, of the Trophy Trout Permit holders are among this group. Others, including many Trout Unlimited members, think the whole stretch should remain catch and release and no fish of any size should ever be killed. There's a rumor going around (and this is just a rumor, mind you) that some of these guys have drawn Trophy Trout Permits, not in order to use them but to keep them out of the hands of those who would.

However you feel about it, you have to admit this is a beautifully subversive, though still legal, tactic, although if it catches on, the Wildlife people will simply figure it into their success-rate calculations and issue that many more permits, leaving the eco-rangers to think of something else.

For the record, the most common criticism of a trophy harvest seems to be that a piece of water tends to adjust itself to the level of the regulations. For instance, just upstream in Spinney Mountain Reservoir you are allowed to keep one trout per day that is 20 inches long or longer—with no special permit required. Consequently, a lot of 19-inch trout are now caught there.

Then again, to be fair to those who feel some fish should be kept, one might ask, What the hell is wrong with a 19-inch trout? Maybe I'm out of step, but to me a fish of that size means photographs, congratulations and then a few minutes of bank-sitting to let it all soak in. Maybe it all comes down to what a D.O.W. biologist once told me, "You can grow big trout with regulations, but you still have to decide what you're gonna *do* with 'em."

I think every fisherman in Colorado knows about the spawning run out of Eleven Mile, and I'd heard many horror stories about the crowds in recent years: shoulder-to-shoulder competitive fishing, a cat's cradle of fly lines whipping dangerously in the wind, a hundred cars in all three parking lots on a weekday, things like that.

I hadn't actually seen it like that for myself, but I'd heard the stories (and you know how easily fishermen buy stories), so I had stayed away for quite a few seasons.

I HAD, along with Mike Price, A.K. and a couple of other friends, fallen into a program of fishing quiet, overlooked, often undervalued places that had to be sniffed out in one way or another. Some were magnificent—real magazine-cover stuff—like the beaver meadows, little trout lakes and pocket water streams we scouted in the mountains. The farm ponds were funkier, but still homey and filled with fish, and there were some ranch tanks with rainbows and brook trout that started out plain, but got prettier as time went by.

I got to be friends with Steve Binder, a good sportsman, bamboo rod and wood canoe expert and all-around nice guy who also just happens to belong to a private trout club.

We were well into the program before we talked about it, but when we did talk, our unofficial motto became "If you've heard much about it, you don't want to go there." We *would* sneak off to famous rivers now and then, for the big trout and the rest of the scene, but it wasn't something we had to explain. Like I said, it was all unofficial, no blood oaths or manifestos, just a handful of fly fishermen showing increased antisocial tendencies.

Then one October came and I realized that I had not blasted off on the road trip to Idaho or Montana or even nearby Wyoming, let alone gotten on a plane for British Columbia. I admit that I missed that part of it and I figure to get back to it, but in the meantime I bought a new tent, camp stove and shotgun with the money I saved.

We decided we were willing to trade fish size for . . . What? Solitude, uncertainty, adventure, whatever you want to call it, but it wasn't even *that* simple, because the hogs—relative or actual—were out there. Like in that farm pond where the bluegills and pumpkinseeds ran up to 13 inches and pushed a pound in weight: astonishing panfish for the western plains. And there was that little lake behind a factory where Mike caught all the big bass and where all I could get were little crappies. And the 16-inch cutthroats in the wilderness area where Mike and I thought we'd see more blue grouse than trout. And the 16-inch brookies in the pond A.K. and I now have a standing invitation to fish.

Okay, but then curiosity, along with a nudge from Engle, got the best of me. Ed doesn't get into these purity trips like I do. When it comes right down to it, he'll pretty much go anywhere and try anything, and then think about it later. He was living close to South Park and had been fishing it some. Now he wanted to see the famous spawning run. We agreed over the phone that there were two time-honored angling rules that applied here:

1. Aesthetics are a major part of fishing. That is, the peace, quiet and solitude are at least as important as the fish. Maybe even more so. And,

2. When the trout are big enough, rule one can be temporarily suspended.

I drove down to Ed's house in Palmer Lake on a Thursday night so we could get a good early start on Friday morning. The weather was cold and snowy, and as we stuffed ourselves on fabulous eggplant parmigiana cooked by Ed's wife, Monica, we talked about how good the fishing conditions would be the next day. Lousy weather almost always equals good fishing, and with a stalled front it was even possible that the wind wouldn't be blowing.

As it turned out, Friday started out chilly, overcast and wonderfully still. A couple of heavy snows would come yet that spring, but that day the floor of South Park was mostly sticky thawed clay under patches of rotting snow, the way you'd expect it to be in May. The mud stuck to the felt soles of our waders, so as we walked out to the river we had to stop and scrape it off every few steps.

Ed suggested we try the upper stretch of the river first. This would be too high up for the spawners—if they were even in yet—but there was supposed to be a good midge hatch there in the mornings.

The midges were on when we got there—right on schedule—and trout were rising in the braided currents below the shallow riffles. There were some other fishermen on the water, but not so many that Ed and I couldn't each find a pod of rising fish. We weren't early enough to get the best spots with the biggest fish in them—places that are well known to the regulars—but there was room for us.

I was within speaking range of another fly caster and we talked while we fished. In a place that's usually packed, you tend to comfortably fish closer to strangers than you would in, say, the Northwest Territories. This man was young, well dressed, clean cut and athletic looking—one of those guys who live on grain and water and run like a horse every day. Not the type to be scared off by South Park's weather. He and I agreed that the crowd wasn't too bad that day.

Naturally, the fish were difficult. I'll never understand what goes on in the cold little brains of the trout, but when they've been fished for a lot they become suspicious in an almost human way, or at least in a way we humans can recognize. A savvy catch-and-release trout will refuse your fly in the same way that a New Yorker will glaze over and walk a little faster when you say, "Hi, I'm from out of town."

I went through three sizes and two colors of emerger patterns, getting inspection rises and refusals to each, and finally began to connect with a #22 pupa pattern fished slightly under the surface. I'd gotten unused to this sort of fishing over the last couple of months, but it came back soon enough. Mostly you just need lots of little flies to try.

I hooked and landed a few good-sized rainbow trout and lost a few others. My biggest fish was about 16 inches—a trout that I couldn't help thinking would be too big to be eaten by even the largest of the spawners that might, at that very moment, be wallowing in the river a couple of miles downstream.

My neighbor grinned when I landed that fish, gave me a clenched-fist salute and said, "Awright." He seemed genuinely happy that I'd caught it.

THAT upper stretch is the only part of this section of river I'd ever fished before—my long affair with the South Platte has mostly taken place many miles downstream in Cheesman Canyon—so after lunch Ed took me on a walking tour of some more water. The river meanders through a wide, open, grassy, flat, usually windswept meadow that reminds me of Montana. There are many tight bends with nice undercut banks on the outside of each one, and some great-looking pools with the ruined buildings of a deserted ranch just barely standing around them. It is very good-looking, very western-looking, trout water.

Looking out across the park from the road, you can't actually see the river. It's only cut a few feet below ground level, but that's enough to hide it until you get close. I've heard that when the good hatches are on you can mark its course by the line of fishermen, but I'd never actually seen *that* for myself, either.

That day there were a number of other fly casters down there, but not too many, considering, and you could have fished anywhere you wanted because the hatch was off and everyone was wandering around aimlessly or having bankside conferences.

Anglers who aren't angling at the moment tend to get friendly, so I ended up talking to some of them. Most said they thought it was surprisingly nice that day. "Not too many people," was a typical comment. I began to wonder what it really means when, in the space of an hour or so, fifteen other fishermen tell you the river isn't crowded.

IF you fish for trout, you're either part of the ongoing debate over hog holes or you've been overhearing it. Your typical hog hole is a blessing and a curse. There are big trout and lots of them, so the fishing is great, but the crowds can be horrifying, so the fishing is lousy.

There are some tricks to fishing hog holes. An old one is to go during nasty, cold, rainy weather, the kind that can scare off fishermen who lack a certain level of dedication. This is an old trick because it doesn't work like it once did. Trout fishing is often at its best when the weather is bad, and modern fly fishermen have become wise in the ways of the sport. They're also pretty tough, despite their yuppie reputations, so a little foul weather doesn't bother them.

You can go during the week, carefully avoiding weekends and major holidays. That doesn't always work, either, but it's at least an even bet.

On the other hand, I spoke with a man not long ago who said the best time to fish a hog hole is *precisely* on holidays like the Fourth of July or Memorial Day. "Everyone assumes they'll be crowded," he said, "so no one goes, and voilà!"

I've never had the guts to try it myself, but I admire that kind of thinking.

If you know the river well, or have a good local source, you can sometimes arrange to slip in at odd times during the season, between the famous hatches that draw the worst crowds. If the place really is a hog hole, the big fish will still be there and they'll still have to eat. As a guide on a famous crowded river once told me of his off season, "There are fewer rising trout now, but there are more rising trout *per fisherman.*"

Sometimes you can camp on site and get in a few uncrowded hours in the early morning while everyone else is driving out from town. Or you can show up late, have a leisurely shore supper while everyone else is leaving and then fish at night. Naturally, this works best in areas where the majority of fishermen day-trip.

When a new hog hole opens up in the same general area as an old one, you can ignore it and keep fishing the old place. With everyone going nuts over the latest hot spot, the crowd on the old river will sometimes thin out significantly for a season or two.

You can become sociable and cagey, as some have done, speaking nicely to all the other fishermen, sharing advice and coffee, while stubbornly staking out your spot in the tradition of the bait fisherman.

Or you can bag the hog holes for the most part and fish the loneliest little creeks, mountain lakes and beaver ponds you can find. That's still possible in the right parts of the country, and I highly recommend it. You'll rediscover a sense of adventure; you'll slow down, chill out, catch some fish, and usually meet few enough other anglers that you'll want to stop and chat with them. Then if you want to hit the big famous river for a change, you can do it philosophically. On bad days you can even feel sorry for the poor saps who think this is fishing.

There are a lot of things you can do, but the problem remains: Many of our best public fisheries are just too crowded. The fish themselves are usually protected to a degree by some kind of tackle restrictions and no-kill or slot-limit regulations, although even that can result in some fish mortality, as well as hook-scarred and otherwise beat-up trout.

And even when the fish fare well enough, the quality of the experience is often badly marred. Fishing is—or should be—a quiet, solitary, contemplative sport. Doing it in a crowd is not unlike taking a shower in a raincoat.

For years there's been talk of solving the problem by somehow limiting the number of fishermen per day on some of our most popular trout streams. The Nature Conservancy has done that on some of their preserves and proved that it has the desired effect, but nothing much has been done yet on public water. To populist-minded American fishermen, limiting access is a distasteful idea, even when we recognize the necessity of it. Some complain about the fees that will surely be part of any limited-access program (the government would bill you for the air you breathe if it could), but mostly it's a matter of principle. This is the United States of America, by God, and public fishing should be free and unlimited.

So, for now at least, many of us have accepted the idea that if we're going to fish some of the country's best and most famous trout streams, we'll have to do it with a lot of company.

Maybe I've mellowed some in recent years, or maybe I just got tired of the lopsidedness of having infinite patience with fish and almost none with my fellow humans, but I'm beginning to get a somewhat different perspective on crowded trout streams. It turns out there is more than one way to look at this.

For one thing, fisheries conservation—as a subheading under conservation in general—is a serious political issue that will only get more important with time. With that in mind I can now sometimes look up and down a river and see not so much a crowd as a constituency: a mob of people that any politician would be happy to see at a rally if they supported him, or terrified to see if they didn't. There are days when I even wish there were two or three more people on the water, like maybe the governor and a couple of congressmen. Not even the President of the United States is immune to what he calls, with typical style, "the environmental thing."

Exchange the politician for an investment banker and another perspective kicks in. Call it environmental economics or, if you prefer, economic environmentalism.

No fly fisherman has to be shown studies to know that large amounts of money are spent on the sport—not just on tackle and licenses, but also on food, travel, lodging, guides, beer and so on. Nor does he have to be told that trout are an indicator species that need cold, clean, unspoiled water.

When most of us look at a hog hole on a normal day, we see a fine piece of trout water that's twenty times more crowded than it should be, but a sharp investment type sees something else: He sees a situation where a healthy natural environment is not an impediment to the development of industry; he sees that in this case a healthy environment *is* the industry.

Yes, I have been hanging out with with some of these guys lately. A lot of them like to fish.

When access is finally limited on some of these waters, most fishermen will see it as a shame, but already some businessmen I know are saying things like, "Wait a minute. You mean you have a product so good you have to turn away customers?"

I cringe at the thought, but if we assume for the moment that wild trout are a product and fishermen are the customers, there are some interesting implications.

For instance, maybe the raving radical environmentalist who was running around a decade ago demanding that the environment be saved and citing truth, beauty and poetry as reasons can now come back and say, "My associates and I would like to show you how minimum flows and special regulations on your stream could bring somewhere between one and three million dollars a year into the local economy."

As an earth-hippie you were treated with strained politeness at best, but now, suddenly, they're calling you "Mister" and paying for your lunch, even though your agenda hasn't changed a bit.

To put it another way, you can make conservation work by convincing people that preserving this forest or that trout stream is the right thing to do, or you can show them that it's not only right, but lucrative.

What we're talking about here is a modest local industry, but it's one that involves no factories, no pollution, no new housing, schools, sewers, water taps, fire trucks, police, etc. Or you can see it as a tourist attraction that doesn't have to turn the town into a carnival and half its citizens into cheap hucksters in coonskin caps. A good trout stream won't bring in the wealth of an oil field, but it will be clean, quiet, dignified, permanent and profitable enough to make looking into the water rights worthwhile.

"Will this actually work?" asks one of the skeptics in the chamber of commerce.

"Well," you can say, "look at that quality stretch of the Such-and-such River. So many people fish it they're trying to figure out how to cut down on the crowds." At that moment you remember being elbowed out of your favorite run fondly, because you can say with conviction, "Trust me, if the trout are here, the people will come."

Hell, they won't even have to advertise. You know how hard it is to keep good fishing a secret.

To many activists, this kind of thing amounts to swimming with the sharks. I suppose it does when you think about it, but it's still possible that the most environmentally meaningful thing you can do right now is teach a banker how to fish and then take him to the jewel in the crown of the state's fisheries on a Saturday afternoon.

From an economic standpoint, this kind of thing requires what can seem like some radical thinking. After all, what we're talking about is existing in some kind of long-term harmony with the natural environment and making a decent living at it, but we're *not* talking about getting fabulously rich overnight. We're looking at the possibility—or maybe I should say the necessity—of being reasonable for a change.

Still (believe it or not) there are some businessmen out

there who understand that our old boom-and-bust, exploit-the-resource-and-move-on program is just not going to work anymore. The problem is, even if you can bring yourself to sanction rape for profit, there's getting to be a crucial shortage of victims.

And I think being reasonable should include us fishermen, too. Unfortunately, some of us have gotten into a kind of junk bond mentality from fishing the hog holes. I've actually talked to guys who won't admit the fishing was "good" unless they were tuna-boating 20-inch trout all day long. But the fact is, many of our best hog holes are tailwater fisheries that have been artificially inflated by the effects of bottom-draw dams. Some of them weren't as good when they were wild rivers, and I know of at least one that held carp instead of trout before the dam went in.

On the other hand, a normal, run-of-the-mill, healthy trout stream that's managed properly with minimum flows and appropriate regulations will likely produce something less spectacular; say, 12- to 14-inch wild, pretty trout with the occasional 16- to 18-inch bomber. Some of us could easily live with that, and maybe a few more of us ought to.

If we spread out a little more, we'll not only have more room to fish, more solitude to enjoy and more new country to see, we'll also spread the tourist dollars around in more businesses in more little towns, and the local chambers of commerce will begin to make the obvious connection: The better the fishing is, the more money they'll make.

It's just conceivable that if we developed all our fisheries to their full potential, the economic benefits would be enough to make it worthwhile. In the end it's a matter of attitude. (Remember that much of life, not to mention some great ideas, depends on nothing more than your point of view.) Crowded hog holes can be seen as proof that the sport is headed for ruin, or they can be used as evidence of just how much a good trout stream is worth in dollars and cents.

And if you measure value in more spiritual and aesthetic

terms, fine. Just between you and me, that's what it really
comes down to in the end. All the rest of this is just a
convenient illusion, but it *is* convenient.

I know this sounds like an oversimplified romantic idea,
but then so did catch-and-release fishing a generation ago. I
know there is at least a handful of businessmen out there who
are beginning to like the economic approach to conservation
(or vice versa), and it's easy to see how this could be used to
lever those politicians who are telling us we can have a
healthy environment *and* a healthy economy. Many of those
guys made that promise off the tops of their heads because it
sounded good. Imagine how relieved they'd be to learn that
it could actually happen.

LATE that afternoon, after hours on the water, Ed and I
headed down below the bridge to look for the spawners. I
realized then that the midge fishing in the morning and the
walking tour of the river had been ways of putting this off.
We hadn't talked about it—Ed and I have kicked around
outside together for so long now that we have finally fallen
silent on some issues—but we do have some misgivings
about fishing for spawners. We've been known to do it, but
we always wonder if it's entirely fair.

Then again, big trout have an almost pornographic appeal,
and these are not only large, but also mysterious. Everyone
knows they come up out of Eleven Mile, but in another very
meaningful way, no one knows where the hell they come
from. They are seldom seen by fly fishers, let alone hooked
and landed, except for those few cold weeks in the off season.
They're hardly ever caught even by the resolute night troll-
ers and ice fishermen who work the reservoirs. For forty-
some weeks out of every year, they might as well be the
ghosts of the old buffalo herds. All the science and technol-
ogy of fishing notwithstanding, there's still that childlike
impulse to catch one of these things and just have a look at
it, whether that's fair or not.

Ed and I weren't holding trophy permits, so at least there wouldn't be *that* question to worry about.

We found some other fishermen down the river, but there weren't too many at that time of day. It had gotten late, it had turned cold and windy, and there were only five or six cars in the lower parking lot. Most of the guys who were left were heading back upstream and all of them gave us the same report: It was pretty dead. There were a few odd fish in, but not many and no really big ones. It was either too early in the year, the river wasn't high enough, the water was too cold and/or the barometer was wrong.

Most of the fly rods we saw were long and heavy—not the light sticks you'd use for midge fishing—and they sported all manner of fly patterns. There were huge streamers, some egg flies (plus one pattern called an Egg-sucking Leech that combines the two) and a few freshwater shrimp patterns. Among those who aren't sure about the ethics of taking spawners are some who feel that if the fish can be caught on real food organism–type flies it's probably okay.

A few hundred yards downriver we came on a pod of half a dozen fishermen. There was a pair of actively spawning trout out on a gravel bar, and one guy was casting to them while the others watched. We watched for a while, too, but it wasn't all that exciting.

Below that spot there was no one. We squinted hard down the meadow where, in that open country, even a distant fisherman stands out like a fence post, but there were no humans in sight, just a mile or so of vacant river. It was four-thirty or five o'clock on a March afternoon in the Colorado Rockies: cold, damp wind; a little snow in the air; dull, gray light; lots of flat space and mountains everywhere you looked.

This was the kind of beautiful desolation Ed and I moved West for in the first place, and also what all those other guys had come to appreciate, each in his own way. Behind us that pod of fishermen had broken up and they were all trudging back to their cars, stopping now and then to knock the mud from their feet. I couldn't be sure at that distance, but no one seemed to be carrying a fish. Probably the guy couldn't get the big one he was trying for, but I hoped he'd caught it—in front of that appreciative audience—and then put it back.

I honestly wished the guy well, and it occurred to me that I had finally negotiated a subtle point: I could dislike a crowd without hating the individuals that make it up. These are my people, after all. In small enough doses they're all good company.

8

SPRING
SNOW

IT COMES EVERY YEAR in April or May: the thick, wet, cling-
ing snowstorm that arrives when the trees have begun to
bud, the early wildflowers are up, Canada geese are on their
nests and spring otherwise seems to have taken hold at an
altitude of 5600 feet in Colorado. For a few weeks, off and on,
the weather has been warm and sweet. I'll have been out for
days already in nothing but shirtsleeves, slathered with 30
SPF sunscreen, resolved to start the season off right in the
solar-radiation department.

It happens every year, but it's still a surprise. One night I open the bedroom window, insert the adjustable screen and begin sleeping with those unidentified, but oddly comforting, outside night noises for company. Three mornings later I'm awakened early by the panicky chattering of a hundred birds at the feeder. My nose is cold, it is snowing heavily, I feel somewhat disoriented.

Some snow has sifted through the screen and there's a damp drift on the inside windowsill, giving the house an abandoned feeling. A sweater and a large pot of coffee seem in order to reestablish a sense of civilization. As an afterthought I go back into the bedroom to close the window.

Only days ago, M. De Witt Daggett III and I were out on the bluegill ponds in our belly boats sampling the spring fishing. The water temperature had risen just enough for the warm-water species to start moving and this was the first real expedition. That is, there had been two previous scouting trips: one with binoculars to just look around and get a feel for things, and one with a fly rod to actually test the waters, to see which of the ponds might fish best that year.

You don't just rush into these things, but this, finally, was the trip with "fish fry" written all over it.

By the book, it goes like this: Spring comes and the water in the ponds warms to the neighborhood of 65 degrees. Then, triggered by the water temperature and, perhaps, the length of the days, the bluegills and other sunfish move into the shallows to spawn. You can usually see their beds in no more than a few feet of clear water. They look like dinner plates or, as someone once said, elephant tracks.

They'll be on the spawning beds for something like a month to six weeks, during which they are easily caught; and during which also the sun shines, days continue to warm and lengthen, trees bud and leaf, migratory birds arrive and so on.

Then, as spring begins to look a lot like summer, the fish finish with their reproductive business and take up their normal warm weather program, which involves feeding in the shallows in the cool mornings and evenings and lounging around in the deeper water during the middle of the day— the aquatic version of picking in the tall cotton.

That's by the book, but, of course, things don't go by the book more than one year out of every three or four, which can get you to wondering about that whole idea of "how things are supposed to be."

De Witt and I tried three ponds, working our way west and south to the one we really wanted to fish. By the time we got there, we already had eight or ten keeper-sized bluegills, spiced up with a few pumpkinseeds and a single rock bass. The bag limit on bluegills being thirty per day, this was just the beginning of a nice mess of fish.

And then there we were at the back end of the good pond. The air was still and warm, but the sky to the west was dark with a thunderstorm, so the light was off the water an hour ahead of schedule. Fish were boiling out on the smooth pond in what was shaping up as an early evening rise. It was working out just right.

We were fishing small weighted wet flies with bodies of peacock herl, and shell backs and tails of pearlescent Flash-abou: the kind of simple, gaudy things bluegills are known to love. We were paddling the float tubes in water that felt only a little cool, catching fish, keeping the good-sized ones and returning the babies so they could grow up.

It was less like a hunt than a harvest. De Witt's mesh creel and my chain stringer were getting heavier to lift, but we hadn't stopped to count the fish yet. If you do this enough, you come to recognize the right heft for, say, a meal of bluegills for two people. Legally we could have kept sixty of them between us. However well it went, we'd stop short of that.

Then the weather began to turn. When it got chilly we stopped to pull on sweaters, when it started to rain we got into slickers, when the thunder and lightning started, we reeled in and quit. A little discomfort in the interest of catching fish is fine—even desirable in some kind of moral sense—

but lightning will kill you, and fishermen are as conscious of that as golfers. You'll even hear discussions of how a bamboo rod, being made of wood, is safer in a storm than a graphite because it doesn't conduct electricity as efficiently.

For the record, if you're hit by 50,000 volts of juice while sitting or standing in the water, the material your fly rod is made of won't make any difference.

So we hiked back to our pickups and I told De Witt to go ahead and keep all the fish. With the harvest called on account of bad weather, there weren't quite enough to split two ways, but this was just the beginning of it. At least six weeks of hot fishing stretched ahead. I could be magnanimous this afternoon, and then come back tomorrow or the next day for some more.

De Witt accepted the fish with thanks, but no argument. There's a sort of logic to these things. I write about outdoor sports for a living (this has been called gratuitous participatory journalism) so I have more time to fish than he does.

As it turned out, that thunderstorm had been stirred up by an advancing low pressure front. The next day was dark and rainy, and the day after that, too, and it got pretty chilly. That went on for a week—cooling the water, putting the fish off—and then it snowed. Somewhere between 5 and 7 inches, depending on the elevation, all of it wet and heavy.

The electricity didn't go off at the house, but I expected it to because it usually does in a big spring snow. I'm on Poudre Valley Rural Electric and I'm a long way from where the power comes from. There are a lot of wires between here and there and one of them usually comes down.

In years past—once I learned what the deal was—I'd simply go onto the backup system: heating with wood, lighting with oil, working on an old manual Royal typewriter instead of the newer electric job, and otherwise feeling like a young Abe Lincoln. But I write on a word processor now and, I'm sorry to say, I can't get along without it, so last spring when the power went off and I just happened to be on a deadline, I drove to town and rented a generator.

This is all perfectly all right, even satisfyingly self-sufficient, except it means that the bluegill fishing has gone to hell.

Not that you worry about the fish themselves. Bluegills—sunfish in general—are a prey species and are, therefore, the toughest little buggers in the lake. Because so many creatures eat them, they need to breed in large numbers to survive as a population. Because they need to breed in large numbers, their spawning requirements are adjustable. When it gets warm enough, they spawn. If it turns cold, they bag it, come back later and try again. They like gravelly or sandy shallows, but if that kind of thing isn't available they'll do it in the weeds like crappies. Eventually they manage it. In latitudes with long growing seasons they've been known to spawn twice for good measure. They're as unstoppably horny as rabbits and even more prolific.

They will eat, or try to eat, just about anything, size notwithstanding, and are in turn eaten, at some point in their lives, by just about every predator in the neighborhood, from dragonfly nymphs to herons to bass to human fishermen. But however many get eaten, there are always more: enough to go around plus enough left over to generate a new crop. In fact, if they aren't slaughtered on a regular basis they'll overpopulate.

Sunfish in general are handsome, if a little on the small side. An individual fish is pretty enough, but they don't get impressive until you've strung up a bunch of them. Then what you have is not so much a quality sporting experience as a meal. Even fly fishermen with their aggravating mystical streaks don't get too misty about sunfish. A bluegill is afforded about the same respect as, say, an ear of corn. These are not considered to be classy game fish (they're too small and too easy to catch) so even scrupulously accurate fly fishers often lump the various species together as "panfish."

It goes without saying that bluegills, and sunfish in general, are delicious. When you're a prey species, tasting good is part of the job description.

The big predator fish in this scenario, the highly respected largemouth bass, is spoiled and delicate by comparison. He requires almost perfect conditions for spawning—a difference in temperature as small as 5 degrees will kill the eggs—and if it doesn't work out that one time he goes off to pout, as if he honestly didn't give a damn about a new generation of bass to carry on. This sort of thing can happen to you when you're at the top of the food chain. You're big enough and fierce enough, but you can come to lack a sense of purpose.

That's why here in Colorado, with our squirrelly weather, the bass have to be helped along with stocking programs—and even then they don't get terribly large—while the sunfish just forge ahead on their own in any clean water that's too warm for trout.

When it comes down to it, it's the meek who inherit the pond.

So it rained and then it snowed, and the bluegills retreated to deep water to wait it out, leaving their spawning beds in the shallows empty for the time being. The electricity didn't go out, as I mentioned, so I could sit home with lights blazing, working on the word processor, with the radio on.

I was sorry I'd given those fish to De Witt. I probably would have eaten them fresh that same night, but if not I could have kept them. The freezer was working and everything.

The day after it stopped snowing I drove up to Susan's cabin in the mountains near here to sow some wild grass seed on what had been a fire line I'd helped to cut the previous year.

That, I think, was a case of instant karma. Earlier that summer I'd been fishing up in the Yellowstone area during the great fires of '88. Some of the locals were freaked out, but

I was among those who were saying, sanctimoniously, "Don't worry, it's supposed to burn, it's the natural ebb and flow." True enough, but easier to say when it's burning toward someone else's motel.

No more than two weeks after I got home, a forest fire started near Jamestown and headed up through the dry woods toward Susan's cabin. I joined the volunteer crew. She's a friend—more than a friend, actually—and I'd spent some pleasant hours in that cabin. And, anyway, I owned a truck and a chain saw and could see the smoke from my front porch.

It was some of the hardest work I'd ever done: sweating, grunting, stopping only to watch the slurry bombers go over, all the time thinking, "Screw the natural ebb and flow. If nothing else, this place is worth a lot of money." When it was all over I had some real difficulty lifting my chain saw onto the tailgate of the pickup.

It was a beautiful fire line. All the trees were cut and the logs and brush were bulldozed off right down to bare, sandy ground. Then, a few hundred yards ahead of it, the fire turned and burned itself out. We had made one hell of a mess out of a pretty mountainside for nothing, and Susan's cabin, once nestled in ponderosa pines, stood out like a new gas station on the interstate.

So that next spring, with a good cover of snow down, a few of us went to scatter some Forest Service wild grass seed to shortcut erosion. Then we had a picnic in the cabin and lay around in front of the fireplace talking. I realized that there were two pretty women, both named Susan, and two bearded men named John: one of those things that seems like it should mean something, but who knows what?

Snow covered the new field outside to a depth of 6 or 7 inches. It looked dirty where we'd scattered the seed. Susan was rubbing the back of my neck absently, and someone (probably just being polite) asked me how the fishing was.

I got into a whole thing about the weather and how it affected the fish. Perhaps I went into too much detail but,

being a fisherman, I'm fascinated by how a natural phenom-
enon like a cold front can change the behavior of certain
creatures and how I can slip into that equation if I've paid
close enough attention. This is not something a lot of people
are into, so it makes me feel outside of things and *right in*
things at the same time. I concluded by saying, "It should
pick up by the end of the week."

At least that's what I'd told Dave Carty when he called to
say he'd be driving down from Bozeman, Montana, to do a
little bluegill fishing with me. "It was on a few days ago," I
said, "and now it's off because of the snow. If the weatherman is right about it warming up, it *should* be back on when
you get here. That's *should, if the weatherman is correct,*" I
added carefully.

But Dave is both persistent and optimistic when it comes
to sporting matters. All he said was, "I have a great beer
batter recipe."

Dave arrived, as he always does, jazzed with enthusiasm
and lugging a cooler full of wild food from Montana: some
Hungarian partridge, a venison roast and a package of frozen
perch fillets. Dave always brings food, probably because he's
a nice, generous guy who's used to pulling his own weight,
although possibly because he's afraid of beef and other people's cooking.

The weather, having been predicted as steadily warming
and clearing, had been fitful and sullen, as if it didn't *want* to
warm or clear. Still, the snow at the elevation of the ponds
had melted, the cottonwoods were budding and new cattail
shoots were coming up, looking stiff, moist and ever so
slightly obscene.

Susan wondered if the grass at her cabin had sprouted yet
and wanted to go up there to check on it. I said it was too
early and, anyway, I was going fishing.

The ponds had muddied a bit from the melting snow,
mostly around the banks, but that had settled out in a day or
two. On the afternoon I'd scouted last—just a quick stop,
sans fly rod—the water still seemed a little cool to the touch,

but the mornings had been bright and the sunlight on the dark pond bottoms would warm the water quickly.

My personal theory on this aspect of the bluegill spawn has to do with lust, a concept I feel I understand. When the fish have been on the spawning beds and are driven off by weather, they are eager to return. As eager as you or I would be, having once been aroused. The *second* the water temperature is right, they'll be back. This is icthyological, but it's still sex, and therefore recognizable.

DAVE and I fished because that's what he'd come to do. If it had been entirely up to me, I'd have waited a few more days. It was the kind of weather you couldn't dress for. It would rain and blow and be chilly. Then it would be calm and the sun would shine for a while—long enough for the pond to become still and for the air to start feeling friendly. Then it would darken and cool and rain again: gray sky, waving grass, running whitecaps on the water, making the cozy little pond look like the North Atlantic.

Our belly boats were set up the same way. One pocket had fly boxes and the general collection of angling odds and ends fly fishers carry, the other had sunscreen, plus wool sweater, gloves and rain gear.

We waited out the worst of the weather in the ruin of a small cinder block building out there that still has half of its roof, and fished between the storms. There's a graffito spray painted on the south wall of this thing now, kind of a shield with horns and eyes. It looks a little like some of the gang stuff I've seen on walls in Denver, but I don't think this is the kind of place where gang members would hang out. Maybe it's art.

The bluegills weren't back in the visible shallows yet, but we located a pod of spawners 60 or 70 yards from shore in about 4 feet of water. They were uniformly good sized—all keepers—and they came easily, bopping the fly hard on a fast retrieve and pretty much hooking themselves.

I know that in a fishing story there's supposed to be more drama to the actual catching, but, as I said, it was easy. We stopped at thirty fish, walked out at dusk and drove home.

It was fun and we were happy to have gone out and killed a bunch of fish to eat. Happy also to have done this with expensive American fly rods fitted with pricey English reels (classic trout tackle) while still somehow avoiding the complicated explanations and philosophizing now required of the fly fisher who kills fish. To wit: Yes, conservation of the resource in the form of catch-and-release fishing is good. And the somewhat pacifistic poetry of sport is good, too, insofar as it civilizes the brutality of mere food gathering. On the other hand, fresh wild food is *good* food: low in fat and cholesterol, without preservatives, tasty and right there in your hand or landing net, free for the taking. Putting too much distance between yourself and such an obvious reality is not productive.

When I was a kid, good fishing didn't have much to do with deep thought. It meant catching lots of big fish quickly and easily on a day when it didn't rain, the wind didn't blow, the mosquitoes weren't too bad and the outboard started on the first pull. "Yes sir, we got our limit and were back on the dock by noon" (with nothing to do for the rest of the day except swill beer and pick lint from our navels, but never mind about that).

Now you're expected to progress upward through the various states of enlightenment from lots of fish, to big fish, to the few truly difficult fish (releasing them all, naturally), until one day your pure soul finally leaves the physical plane altogether in a flash of blue light, leaving behind nothing but a pair of singed hip boots.

To some modern purists, the frying of a few fish is a small but meaningful act of heresy, which, aside from the culinary experience, is why some of us like to do it. Of course, we'd sidestepped the issue a bit by frying bluegills, which are a real blue-collar fish: easy to find, easy to catch, good to eat, period. I'm surprised they don't serve them at truck stops.

The true fly-fishing rebel would kill and eat wild trout, but that's a whole other story.

DAVE does bluegills up beautifully. The small fillets are dipped in beer batter, which is one part white flour, one part cornstarch, a pinch each of salt and baking powder, plus the beer. It's quite possible that the actual brand of beer makes no difference at all, but, in the interest of fine-tuned sensibilities, use something like Corona instead of Bud Light.

The battered fillets are deep fried in oil. Peanut oil is best, but vegetable oil will do. When each batch is browned, they go into a strainer that's placed over a bowl in a 200 degree oven. This keeps the fillets warm until the whole batch is done, and also tends to percolate out the excess oil, which collects in the bowl, so they're not too greasy. Serve with salad, corn bread and more Mexican beer.

The next night Dave would cook a perch and venison feast for some friends, including the two lovely Susans, but we ate that first mess of bluegills by ourselves, with our fingers, in the kitchen.

And we did what free-lance writers traditionally do when they haven't seen each other in a while: We bitched about editors, deadlines, work loads and money. Dave typically has a lot to say on these matters and he's not shy about it. Among certain writers and outdoor types, saying exactly what you mean regardless of the consequences is now known as "pulling a Carty."

Then, with the preliminaries out of the way, we settled down to what's wrong with the world outside of our own little universe of discourse. What's wrong, we believe, is that there's too much distance between humans and our natural environment. Most of us want things to be at least at arm's length. We don't like to touch things that haven't been sanitized; we don't care for food that doesn't come wrapped in plastic; we don't even like to walk on surfaces that haven't been specially prepared for that purpose, and the pitiful shoes many of us wear reflect that fact.

And fly fishermen, now more skilled and knowledgeable than they've ever been, seldom keep any of the fish they go to such pains to catch. There are sound reasons for that, but the sport has become a highly refined, ritualistic food-gathering technique in which damned little food is gathered. But then maybe that's how we do things now.

We agreed that how a culture relates to and encounters nature is the only valid criterion for judging its quality. On the way back from the ponds we had passed some enormous radio telescopes that I understand are used by SETI—the Search for Extraterrestrial Intelligence. These people send messages out into the cosmos (essentially, "Hey, we're here. Are you there?") and then listen for some kind of reply.

When we do finally make contact, there's only one question we'll have to ask to learn all we need to know about the space brothers: "Do you guys fish?"

As I see it, there are only four possible answers: "Yes," "No," "We used to, but the fish are all gone now," or "What is fishing?"

By midnight we had eaten, drunk and talked too much, somehow becoming one with nature in the process. We decided we were frontier subsistence journalists, living off the land in one of the few ways that's still possible, that is, by gathering food, putting most of it back and then writing about it for money. Maybe this is partly an illusion, but it does put you outside every morning, squinting up at the sky like a farmer, not just looking at the weather, but having some inkling of what it means.

It had started snowing again, lightly this time, and, although it wasn't a terribly cold night, we started a fire in the wood stove just for the pure joy of burning some pine.

9

DOGS

THE MAIN REASON FOR A RECENT TRIP to Montana was to do a little trout fishing, but in the course of going around and seeing fishermen I also met some pretty snazzy bird dogs. Not that the people weren't impressive in their own way, but you meet people all the time.

Now I don't have much expertise in this area. All of the hunting dogs I've had were hounds who were into the well-worn hound program, that is, they chased things and bayed,

period. If I wanted to follow along behind with a gun, doing
my best to keep up, that was my lookout. You don't "work"
a hound, you just turn him loose and, if anything, he works
you. I've never owned a bird dog and wouldn't begin to
know how to train one, but I've hunted with some fine ones
and I'm just smart enough to know when to be impressed.

Naturally, I already knew Fancy and Poke, belonging to
Carty, whom I stayed with for a while. Poke is a springer—a
flushing dog—and Fancy is a Brittany, a pointer. These are
both dogs I know well and have hunted with, so it's always
good to see them. Good to see Dave too, of course, although
compared to the dogs' his greeting always seems to lack
enthusiasm.

Poke is an excellent springer: a smart, dedicated hard
worker who will hunt until he drops, although he has a
hardheaded or perhaps even slightly crazy streak. He's been
described as a little tank, also as a mad genius.

Poke can get pheasants out of the thickest cover and he has
made some heroic retrieves in his day—dodging ice floes in
swift, cold rivers to run down crippled ducks, that sort of
thing. On the other hand, he has this tendency to escape from
his kennel and get into all kinds of inventive trouble around
the neighborhood. For some reason, he likes to crap on a
certain neighbor's back porch. He'd rather hunt, but if he
can't do that he has to do *something*. Poke has never been one
to lounge around on the front porch looking rustic.

He will ride quietly and politely in his mobile kennel in the
back of Dave's pickup as long as you're on a paved road, but
as soon as you turn onto dirt or gravel he starts to howl. He
will do this for miles, never getting tired or hoarse. A dirt
road, you see, means you're almost there, at least in the literal
mind of a springer spaniel.

In other words, whatever you can say about Poke that's
good, something else comes to mind that's not so good.

Dave is an outdoor writer specializing in bird hunting, so
Poke has been trained to pose proudly and handsomely for

photographs, holding anything in his mouth that you care to hand him: a grouse, a beer can, it doesn't matter to Poke. In Montana this amounts to high-class entertainment.

I hunted with Fancy last fall in her first bird season. She was just eight months old then, but she was already ranging widely and pointing beautifully. Every now and then she'd decide to go into a classic point on a cow pie—for reasons known only to herself—but based on what little I know of bird dogs I think that can be written off as basic puppy goofiness.

Dave thought Fancy made a few mistakes that first season, like not always waiting for the command before retrieving a bird (once she ran out and caught a dead partridge before it even hit the ground), but all her mistakes came from enthusiasm rather than stupidity, and for a pup she was brilliant. Dave allowed as how she showed some promise. Every time he talks about her he beams like a proud father.

Fancy will also hunt till she drops, and then, given half a chance, she'll drop in your lap, after giving you a couple of big kisses. As a breed, Brits are happy and affectionate dogs, but Fancy is shameless.

Fancy is a dog I'd steal if I had the chance. I like Poke a lot too, and I love to hunt with him, but I'm glad he belongs to someone else.

Now Dave travels in some pretty serious gun dog circles, and one day he took me out to meet a friend of his. When we went to the door we were met by a pretty Brittany (for partridge and quail), a big, happy black Lab (for waterfowl) and an elegant English setter (pheasant and grouse). All this guy would need to qualify as the ultimate dog maniac would be a terrier for rats.

These dogs were hanging around in the house unashamedly, and the man made no apologies for that, which I liked. Sometimes when you show up somewhere unexpectedly and the dogs are lying on the furniture, the guy will say something like, "I usually don't let 'em in the house," and hustle the dogs out to an apparently seldom-used kennel behind the garage. The dogs will look puzzled by this, while back in the house, you notice old dog-shaped impressions on the couch and easy chair.

Where the dogs should stay is not something I have strong opinions on. I will say, however, that the best bird dogs I've known seemed to spend more free time in the house with the people than behind chain link in the back yard. They were good hunters and good company, too.

I hadn't seen an English setter in years and I'd forgotten what a lovely dog this was: tall, slim, fast-looking, feathery ears and tail, freckles. Very Old World. Dave and his Montana friends train their dogs with live birds, and all I had to do for this guy to produce a pigeon for the demonstration was admire the dog.

The setter worked quickly—frantic but still methodical—and as soon as she got downwind of the bird she froze into a textbook point, skidding to a stop in the damp grass. The man did not look at me to make sure I was appreciating this fully. He looked at the dog and grinned.

I love the expressions pointers get on their faces when they have a bird. Some seem to be struggling to contain themselves, fighting off the idea that they could handle this better than the guy back there with the shotgun. Some seem puzzled, even cocking their heads, and others will glance over their shoulders to see what's taking you so damned long to get there, which I understand is bad form.

The best, like this setter, seem to be balanced between pure joy and perfect anticipation, thinking, Okay, I've done my part, now it's the hunter's turn. If he misses I'm gonna give him a look that would wilt an oak tree.

There are whistled and spoken commands, hand signals, even meaningful glances, but beyond that there is often a kind of telepathy. The dog and the hunter know each other, they're not just pieces in a game.

In the ideal scenario the dog is well trained (that is, well trained before the fact, not yelled at and scolded in the field) and the human is stern, but also patient and willing to relinquish control at the proper times. In those cases where the human is smarter than the dog, the dog is usually willing to act accordingly. At its best the relationship is less like a slave and a master, more like a junior and a senior partner.

Let's be honest. It's like two specialists: a team too small to need a captain.

It's a truly fine sight to see a human and a dog working together. It's also fine to be part of the scene yourself, along for the ride with someone else's good dog. You get all the benefits except one: that warm flush of pride. Since it's hard not to get corny about this, I'll just say it: This is the deep satisfaction that comes from watching a worthwhile job being done well. It's the kind of thing that can give you hope for the future of both species, and when I see it I feel nothing less than pure, green envy.

David Quammen, the nature writer, doesn't care for dogs. He thinks there are too many of them, that whatever admirable qualities they may once have had have been bred out of them and that they bark too much to be useful as watchdogs. "Who would depend on an alarm system that gives twenty false alarms a day?" he asks.

He's probably right about most pet dogs, but working dogs have a purpose in life, and if they're a pain in the ass when they're not in the field, at least there's a good reason why you should put up with that.

Many hunting dogs *are* high strung, and some of them have some odd, almost human quirks. There's the story of an enormous Chesapeake Bay retriever who is, it's said, one of the great waterfowl dogs of all time, but every now and then he'll stop on his way back to the blind and eat the duck he's carrying. He figures he deserves it, and no one ever tries to stop him.

Dutch, Larry's little German shorthair, has turned out to be a good dog in the field and excellent company at home or in camp, but when he's riding in the car and sees another dog, he likes to mark his territory by peeing on the upholstery.

Dog people just live with things like that, and when you think about all the crap we civilized humans have had to learn to put up with, it's not much of a stretch. Larry's wife, Donna, said recently that she'd been trying to teach Dutch some manners, but she didn't act like it would be a tragedy if it didn't work. I asked her if she was going to start on Larry when she finished with the dog. She said she was good, but not that good.

LATER in the trip, over by Big Timber, Montana, where I got permission to fish a private stream, I met a young black Lab who was typically jolly and friendly. Some hunters like Labs and some don't, but it's hard to find someone who doesn't think they have sweet dispositions. The guy said this dog would probably go fishing with me and then brought up something I'd said once in a book.

What I'd said was, there is no such thing as a good fishing dog, whatever the owner of said dog tells you. The worst wade ahead and trash the water or try to retrieve the fish, while the best sit on the bank emitting a pitiful, high-pitched whine all day.

I should have known I'd meet a good fishing dog no more than a year after I wrote that, and I did. His name was Tucker, a retired golden Lab who used to live with Roy Palm over on the Frying Pan River in Colorado. Tucker didn't get in the way, didn't try to retrieve the fish, and didn't whine and whimper all day, which is really all it takes to be a good fishing dog, although very few can actually manage it. This dog would simply lie on the bank and watch Roy fish. When Roy got too far away, Tucker would lurch to his feet, hobble a few yards upstream and lie back down again.

Whenever Ray hooked a trout, which was often, Tucker would lift his head from his paws and wag his tail—slowly.

Tucker was very old then—in fact, he's no longer with us now—and I just figured he was a good dog because he didn't have the strength left to be a bad one.

But the black Lab in Montana was young and frisky and I figured I was in for some grief.

When I got down to the stream the Lab was right at my heels, and he was excited about going fishing. In fact, he'd been excited ever since he saw me string up the fly rod. His first choice would have been to go duck hunting, of course, but this was going to be okay. There'd be cold water and maybe a little action. It would be better than nothing.

I'm smart enough not to kick the dog belonging to the man who's just let me onto a fine piece of water that few people ever fish (for the record, I'm not a dog kicker in any event), so I tried to explain the rules.

"Now I'm gonna wade out here and fish," I said in the most serious voice I could manage. "I want you to stay behind me"—I pointed, the dog looked—"stay quiet, and don't try to grab the trout, okay?"

The dog looked me in the eye and nodded once.

To make a long story short, the Lab was a perfect gentleman. He followed at a respectful distance, he never made a sound, and every time I'd hook a fish he'd just wag his tail and perk up his ears. He'd have gotten into the act if I'd invited him to, but as it was, he was happy enough to watch.

It was actually pretty pleasant. I like to fish alone, but it was nice to have some silent company: another organism to watch me hook and land a good trout and, I believe, understand the significance of it.

I caught a lot of fish and when I finally quit I patted the Lab on the head and said, "You're a good boy."

He gave me a level, dignified look. This was a dog who knew he was a good boy and didn't have to be told so by some stranger who was fishing on his stream.

Later I ended up on the porch of the house talking with my host, where I had to admit that, yes, there *are,* in fact, a few good fishing dogs, although I still maintain they're few and far between.

With the fun over, the Lab had wandered off somewhere, but there was an old pointer sleeping at the man's feet and a young one larking around out in the grass. We were talking about cutting horses (if there's anything I know less about than bird dogs it's cutting horses) when the pup snapped into a picture-book point not 20 feet in front of us.

"What's she got there?" I asked, thinking maybe this guy had Hungarian partridge living in his front yard.

"A butterfly," the guy said matter-of-factly, "but I think she's gonna grow out of that."

10

BAMBOO

S TEVE BINDER IS THE MOST dedicated bamboo rod collector I know. For a while he said he honestly didn't know
how many rods he owned, then, not long ago, he said he
realized that was some kind of avoidance tactic, so he
counted them. At the time there were around fifty. He hasn't
fished all of them because they're coming in too fast, but he's
working on it. I've never been out with him when he didn't
have a trunkful of rod cases, and I'm not sure I've ever seen

him fish the same rod twice, although one gets confused in this blur of varnished bamboo.

Steve is the kind of fisherman who'll ask, "If you could only have fifteen rods, what would they be?"

He told me he got into this not to amass a world-class collection or to make a profit (although a profit can be made if you know what you're doing) but just to learn about the rods because he liked them and was curious and had the money to buy them.

I believe that. I've only known Steve for a few years, but he seems like the type who'll dig into something that strikes his fancy and come out a few seasons later somewhere between a topflight amateur and a pro, just for the sheer hell of doing it.

I once suggested that to his wife, Sharon, and she said I had no idea how true that was. There's probably a story there. Probably none of my business.

Last July Steve invited me up to his cabin at the Kenosha Trout Club for what sounded like a theme fishing trip. Bobby Summers, the famous rod maker from Traverse City, Michigan, was flying out to fish with Steve, and they'd decided to make it a party. Two other well-known rod makers, Charlie Jenkins and my friend Mike Clark, were going to show up, as well as me and Bill Vidall, not collectors in Steve's league, but definitely accumulators and users of bamboo rods.

I try never to pass up a chance to fish this great private lake from the comfort of Steve's old but posh cabin, and I figured I could pick up all kinds of esoteric, inside stuff about bamboo fly rods if I could just keep my mouth shut and listen. It sounded like a good group—if a little too big—and, yes, it also sounded pretty high tone.

There's an atmosphere of classy sport around Binder's cabin that I find hard to resist. It's not just the lake full of brook trout. Steve has set this thing up so that everything exudes either quality or the proper amount of funk, from the food and booze to the art on the walls to the surprisingly comfortable rocking chairs built like wood-and-gut snowshoes. Naturally, there's no telephone. Bamboo rods—reeking of tradition as they do now—fit right into that.

A.K. was invited, but, because of unspecified prior commitments, he would have time either for the Trout Club or the Green Drake hatch on the Frying Pan River, but not both. He would have loved to immerse himself in bamboo rods, talk and brook trout at a classy cabin in the woods for a few days, but, typically, he was more jazzed about dry fly fishing on the Pan, sleeping in his tent and eating canned Dinty Moore stew with hickory salt.

As I said, the prior commitments were not explained. In this group, the assumption is you'll go. If you can't, no one asks why for fear the reason would seem too trivial.

So it was decided that A.K. would go camp on the Pan at our usual spot behind Roy Palm's place in about a week, and I and anyone else who wanted to would join him after we finished at the lake.

Then we decided none of this would be right if Ed wasn't there, so he agreed to drive up from Palmer Lake and meet us on the Pan on or about a certain day.

Steve's son Cass would probably show up at some point, and it wasn't clear how much of this he, Vidall, Charlie or Mike would be in on. I tried to keep it all straight for a while, then decided I wasn't in charge, so I didn't have to worry about it.

Finally, A.K. called Roy over on the Pan to ask if he minded having a slightly larger mob than usual camping on his property. No, A.K. said, we didn't know exactly how many, but this was beginning to look like the trip that takes on a life of its own. Roy said he understood, having been on a few like that himself.

I talked to some friends who bring in my mail and feed my cats while I'm gone; said I didn't know exactly when I'd be back. That was okay, they said, "We aren't going anywhere for a while."

I filled the saddle tanks on the pickup with 32 gallons of gas, strapped the canvas canoe on the roof, threw in the float tube just in case, and checked the camper for the tents, tarps, camp stove, coolers, food boxes, water jugs and such that are always supposed to be in there, ready to go. Then came waders, flies, fly-tying kit, reels, and five or six of my best bamboo rods.

I had discussed which rods I should bring with A.K. like a schoolgirl deciding on what dress to wear to the dance. A.K., always the pragmatist, said, "Bring the rods you'll use and then throw in a couple of pretty ones."

I MET Binder and Bob Summers at the cabin. Actually, they passed me a few miles from the dirt road turnoff and I chased them the rest of the way. I'd been driving slowly, enjoying the kind of dreaminess I get into now at the beginning of long trips with no clear end.

I met Summers as he held the gate open for me at the club. Steve set about the practiced ritual of opening up the cabin, while Bob and I unloaded gear. At some point cold beers appeared. Then Mike Clark's big white fishing van with the belly boat rack on top eased down the drive. There were more introductions, more beers and more people trickled in. As fishing expeditions go, the atmosphere was more social and less, shall we say, "businesslike" than I'm used to. Still, it wasn't long before rods were strung, canoes were launched and fish were caught.

And then Steve was firing up this thing that looks like a cross between a propane tank and a jet engine and cooking his famous Cajun blackened steaks. Until I met Binder, I didn't like blackened food—I thought Cajuns were an unfortunate race of people who couldn't sing and couldn't cook— but Steve is one of the few who can burn the meat just right.

For the next few days some people came and went—Cass

showed up late, Charlie Jenkins had to leave early, etc.—and we fished with, cast and talked about bamboo rods, sometimes far into the night. I don't know how many rods were there. Charlie, typically modest, showed up with two of his, and he'd have only brought one to fish with if Steve hadn't wanted to look at the other one.

Summers, out of his Michigan element and not knowing what to expect, had brought a pretty good stack of his rods, from short and light to long and heavy.

Mike Clark was also well represented. He had a couple of his own rods, Binder had one and I had two. If I remember right, Vidall ordered a rod from Mike on, or just after, this trip.

And there were some Grangers, Heddons, Winstons, Leonards, a Pezon et Mechelle, a Thomas & Thomas, a couple of Dickersons, and I don't know what all else. A rod would come out of its tube to be admired, and then we'd all naturally have to go down to the dock and try it. All of us, that is, who hadn't wandered off to catch brook trout.

Then another rod would be brought out for comparison, which would remind someone of another rod he'd brought, and so on into the afternoon. There were graceful, demanding parabolics; delicate, weightless midges; crisp dry fly rods; thunderstick western wind rods.

As you might expect, the three rod makers were thoughtful casters. They'd false cast a new rod tentatively, cocking their heads as they felt it load, then watching the loop over their right shoulders, not forcing themselves on it, but waiting for the rod to show them what it wanted, then saying something like, "Uh-huh," or maybe, "Ah."

Every now and then trout would start rising within range of the dock and someone might think to tie on a fly.

When one of the guys who'd gone off to fish wandered back to the cabin, someone would say, "Did you get a chance to cast Mike's eight-and-a-half-foot six-weight?" and the whole thing would start all over again. There were rods lying in canoes, on the dock, on the picnic table, propped against trees, and hung on the inside and outside rod racks at the cabin. Somehow, none got stepped on.

One of Charlie's rods, a 7-foot 3-weight, was the very one that had come in second in some kind of bamboo rod competition that was held by the Anglers Club of New York a few years ago. I tried it out on the dock. It was a sweet rod in every way, and I'm sure it and Charlie deserved the honor, but I, for one, would never be able to judge an event like that: objectively rating one good rod above another, and then telling other people what I'd decided as if that actually meant something.

Rods are like books. I can usually tell quality from junk, but the idea of rightness is harder to pin down and impossible to defend. For instance, if you happen to like John Updike's novels better than those of Jim Harrison, as some deluded easterners do, what could I possibly say to make you feel otherwise?

I did eavesdrop on the three rod makers a few times and, after talking with Mike off and on for quite a few years, I should have known what to expect. Aside from sheer castability and workmanship, Binder comes at rods in terms of their history and collectible status, while I think more about warmth and tradition, but the rod makers talked about glues and varnishes, planes and forms and milling machines and heat treating and where to get good stripping guides: the nuts and bolts of it that, I have to admit, don't interest me all that much.

The secrets I had envisioned learning boiled down to one: that these guys were simply working craftsmen with an abiding interest in the details of their jobs. They're not gurus, and they seem a little puzzled by the fishermen who want them to be.

It actually seems like a fair division of labor. Those of us who use bamboo rods—sometimes spending more than we can afford to get them—formulate the poetry and the romance, while the makers simply work to build the best fishing poles they're capable of.

. . .

WHEN things got too technical, I'd go out and catch brookies. The fish have their moments there, but mostly they are
friendly, easy trout that will bop a weighted Hare's Ear
nymph or Elk Hair Caddis dry fly that's fished with any
attention at all.

I've never done as well there as Mike did one afternoon
when he stood in one spot down at the outlet and caught no
less than forty trout, but I was doing well enough that I
found myself airing out rods I'd brought to show off rather
than to fish, just to remember how they felt with a trout on.

We ate well at the cabin: steaks, spaghetti, hot green chili
and, one day, an incredible mess of brook trout. The club's
management strategy had recently turned from numbers of
fish to trophy size, and to that end they wanted the larger
brookies thinned out heavily. So one morning we all duti-
fully set out to kill lunch. I'm an advocate of catch-and-
release fishing (about 98 percent, as Mike says) but I've
found that in recent years I'm more and more delighted by
an excuse to kill and eat wild fish. They're just so damned
good and, yes, they're noticeably better when caught on a
bamboo rod.

The trout were butterfly filleted, slathered with butter and
herbs, quickly grilled and served with beer and potato salad.
I don't know how many fish there were, but they stuffed
seven grown men to the point where we were all staring at the
last two saying, "No, go ahead."

One night, to get a taste of local society, we drove to a
roadhouse not far down the highway that's patronized
mostly by people driving large, black motorcycles. It was a
cozy, friendly place with a resident Doberman who seemed
to recognize the smell of fishermen. On the only other automobile in the parking lot, there was a MADD (Mothers
Against Drunk Drivers) bumper sticker. Inside, the bar-
tender was wearing a DAMM (Drunks Against Mad Mothers) T-shirt. The food was great.

. . .

THE next afternoon we pulled into Roy's place on the Frying Pan. Some people had dropped off in the days we were at the cabin, and when the trip finally shifted into Phase Two it was down to Binder, Summers and me in two vehicles.

A.K.'s camp was set up when we arrived. It was typically snug and efficient: fire, shelter, light, food and a cooler of Coors Light laid out more or less in order, designed for quick escapes in the mornings and lounging in the evenings. A.K. himself was off fishing.

Ed wandered in later that day, and by the time we headed out to fish the evening hatch there were four pickup trucks parked as discreetly as possible back in the trees, a circle of tents facing a fire pit, A.K.'s elaborate camp kitchen, which is known locally as "the A.K. Box," a folding camp table compliments of Binder, aluminum lawn chairs, a stack of firewood covered with a tarp and, of course, Roy's dogs.

There's always a changing roster of retrievers here, Chesapeakes, usually, and they always move right in to the current fishing camp. This time it was our old friend Teal—now semiretired and a little gimpy—and an adolescent Chesie named Gus. Gus didn't understand what was going on, but he seemed eager to learn.

When Roy came home from his fly shop down in Basalt, he wandered out to say hello and said it looked like a tribe of Gypsies had moved in on him. I don't know exactly how he meant that, but I liked the sound of it.

The fact is, enough visitors camp here in a given year that Roy recently erected a palatial outhouse. Before the cement stoop was dry, he scratched "Dedicated to friends and fishermen" in it with a stick. It occurred to me that this might just be self-defense against having God knows how many visiting fishermen shitting God knows where around the place all summer, but I finally decided it was just one more example of Roy's considerable class and generosity.

The running bamboo rod discussion had actually begun to

peter out over the last couple of days—it's a bottomless subject, but it's possible to get numb, and there are, after all, fish to be caught. But then that first evening on the Pan, with some new people, and some new rods, it started up again, and Roy, who I'd never seen fishing anything but a graphite, went up to the house and came back with a lovely little 7½-foot Gary Howells, so as not to be outdone.

THE whole bamboo rod business can get pretty complicated. Among the old rods there are legitimate museum pieces; a whole range of collectibles from rods by acknowledged masters like Payne, Garrison and Gillum down through many other individual makers; to Leonards, which, for some reason, seem to be in a high-priced class by themselves; to the good production rods like the Heddons and Grangers; merely decent production rods like South Bends and Shakespeares; real antiques; some curiosities and some out-and-out junk.

Among the new rods are those made by companies like R. L. Winston, Orvis and Thomas & Thomas; rods built by dozens of independent makers now working around the country—ranging from famous masters to unknown hobbyists—and some imports.

And then there are obscure models, special models, limited editions, one-of-a-kind custom rods perhaps built for celebrities, rods made by one company but with another company's name on them, vintage nameless rods of various quality made by who knows who, the T&T rod built for the prime minister of Australia and so on. As I said, it's a bottomless subject.

Somewhere in there you cross the fuzzy line between fishing rods and collector's items, and that's what clouds things up. That and money. I hesitate to get into actual figures because they change constantly, but I'm the one who brought it up, so here goes.

For between $700 to $1,600 you can get, at this writing, all

kinds of new and used production rods, new and used contemporary handmade rods and a fair range of collectibles.
Some of the rods in this group will increase in value sooner
and more spectacularly than others. Damned few will lose
their value, assuming they don't get slammed in car doors.

There are some good, usable fly rods for less than that,
although many of the old, quality production rods that were
once affordable are being sucked into the vacuum left by the
top-of-the-line collectibles, some of which are now going for
five figures.

Discussions of money are unavoidable when it comes to
bamboo rods because they *are* expensive and there are precious few real bargains left. A good, usable bamboo fly rod will
now cost you between twice and five times the price of a
top-quality graphite, and therein lies much of the mystique.

In some circles, how little you paid for a rod is a matter of
status. In other circles it's how *much*. I've been told of brag-
ging matches where one collector says, "I fish my $3,000
Payne," and another counters, "Well, *I* fish my $6,000 Gar-
rison. So there."

If by "fish" they mean they took it to a nearby stream once
and caught a few little trout just to see what all the fuss over
Payne and Garrison was about, okay. Anyone would do that.
But if they mean they threw it in the pickup and took off for
a couple of weeks in Idaho, I don't know if I believe it, or if
I'm impressed.

It's like the guy who made the news a few years ago for
paying half a million dollars for a bottle of wine at auction.
"What are you going to do with it?" the reporters asked.
"I'm gonna drink it," he answered.

One hopes, depending on one's opinion of the idle rich,
that it was either damned good or that it had turned to
vinegar.

I GUESS the collecting end of bamboo rods interests me
because I have the same morbid fascination everyone has

with rare old items costing large amounts of money, and because some of the used rods I bought to fish with not too many years ago are now beginning to appear in the rod lists well out of my price range. But I really just like to fish them, and so I wish they weren't so expensive.

Then again, you have to look at that from the proper perspective. Let's say a good rod maker builds you a hand-made bamboo fly rod for $800—a more or less reasonable price these days. He's probably put about forty hours into it; his raw materials and parts are expensive and sometimes hard to find; he's got tools and machines to buy and maintain; rent on the shop; plus all the odds and ends that accumulate in a small business, like stationery, business cards, brochures, advertising, shipping and whatever else. Not to mention screwed-up blanks that get broken up and tossed in the wood stove, bad checks and the years he probably spent learning how to do this, during which he didn't make a penny and spent at least a small bundle to get set up.

In the end, you're looking at a highly skilled, self-employed craftsman who's pulling down $8 or $10 an hour at best, which, to me, does not seem unreasonable.

To put it another way, it's your lawyer and your doctor who drive BMWs and vacation in the Bahamas, not your rod maker.

I picked a lot of this up from hanging out with Mike. I met him years ago when he was just starting to make bamboo rods. He was working nights and weekends in a friend's wood stove–heated garage, hand-planing rods and financing the whole thing by operating heavy equipment. He reminded me of some starving artists and writers I've known.

I'll spare you the full-length sob story. It's enough to say he worked long and hard, burned up a lot of unsuccessful blanks in the stove, spent his rare days off fishing prototype rods to see how they acted and didn't start selling rods until they were good, even though people had begun to pester him, and even though he probably could have used the money. I got the third one he made for sale, a few years later

I got a second one and now he's making me that 7 foot 9 incher.

For a long time Mike was an unusual rod maker in that he only did custom work—no standard models. He'd work out length, line weight and action with each new customer, and then he'd ask the guy what kind of reel seat, spacer and color of wraps he wanted; whether the hardware should be blued or shiny; whether he wanted a hand-rubbed tung oil or a varnish finish and so on. In the end, no two rods were alike. This cost Mike more in time and materials, so his profit margin was lower, but he said it was more fun that way.

Mike still does mostly custom work, but he has finally allowed himself to develop a handful of more or less standard models, if only because so many people have asked him to reproduce certain rods. I'm proud to say some of those were first made for me and A.K. It's not that we had much to do with their design, but we did ask Mike to build them.

Because so many of Mike's rods are unique (and because he's getting to be well known), some collectors are already interested in him. In the grand scheme of things, his prices are still reasonable, but the day will probably come when he joins those few contemporary rod makers whose rods are collector's items before the varnish is dry. When that time comes he may be able to drop another new engine in the van.

ONE evening on the Frying Pan, A.K. said it was a relief to be in a group where no one was asking, as some people do, "Why do you guys fish those old wood rods?"

I knew what he meant, but I actually like it when people ask that. Fishermen are usually fairly crazy, and their main goal in life is to grow up to be even crazier yet, so when one of these nuts walks up to me and asks why the hell I'm doing what I'm doing, I feel like I'm really out there—well on my way to becoming the cosmic old fart.

But the social implications are a side benefit. The fact is, when compared to graphite, bamboo is better in every way for the kind of fishing I do, that is, casting at normal ranges with light- to medium-weight rods for trout, bass and panfish.

A bamboo rod loads more naturally and reacts more organically to the whims of the caster. It's also more forgiving than graphite, so in the end it's much easier to cast well if you're not an expert. People worry about the slight extra weight, but all that does is make the rod work more while you work less so that, even though a comparable graphite is lighter, I find it more tiring to cast. And I'd hate to hear what our forefathers—who fished 10-foot solid greenheart rods weighing a couple of pounds—would say to all this whining over a couple of ounces.

I find that a good bamboo rod will mend line with more authority, cushion light tippets better and play fish with more stubborn guts than any graphite I've tried.

For sheer sensuality of casting and for fishing that requires some subtlety, a good bamboo rod is simply the superior instrument, so it doesn't really bother me that it costs several times what a graphite does, because it's several times better.

Not that I'm what you'd call a stickler for quality in general. In fact, my life tends to operate on the "good enough" principle most of the time, but fly-fishing is what I love the most and have stayed with the longest, so it seems logical to do it with the finest tools I can afford—or not afford, as the case may be. The fact that my house, clothes, pickup and such don't live up to that model only seems to make the rods stand out more brilliantly by comparison.

And they are just plain beautiful, which I think is why collectors have glommed onto them while pretty much ignoring rods made from other materials, however old or historically interesting they might be.

I've considered getting into collecting as such myself, and after talking about it with Binder for a couple of years, I can see how it might be fun: buying some rods that aren't too pricey right now—but that I've guessed will evolve into the next generation of Gillums and Garrisons and just stashing them away for ten years to see if I guessed right.

I mentioned that to Ed one afternoon while we were sitting around drinking coffee, and he asked me if I really wanted to get into taking great fly rods out of circulation and hiding them until they were worth so much no one would ever fish them again.

Ed does that. He's an intellectual saboteur who will make you examine your own thinking with a critical eye whether you want to or not.

Ed and I do have somewhat different visions of the world. I once told him that if I couldn't fish with fine tackle, I might not fish at all. He said he'd fish if they made it illegal and he had to do it at night with a pitchfork. Be that as it may, I still usually find his logic inescapable.

We talked about it for quite a while, getting into things like how human beings attribute value, the morality of turning a profit through inaction, what you're really doing when you take something that could be part of your real life and turn it into a monument, etc., and, Ed finally convinced me—or helped me to convince myself—that I should simply buy the rods I wanted to fish if I could afford them, and if they ended up worth a fortune someday it would give my surviving relatives a nice surprise.

And it isn't all about money, either. There's a lot of good, honest nostalgia connected to bamboo rods. Mike Sinclair once showed me a sweet old 10-foot Orvis rod from about 1890. It was a handsome rod with a sheet cork grip, red intermediate wraps, sliding band reel seat with a maple spacer, but the best thing about it was, it had old, dried trout scales stuck in the varnish on the butt section. You've got to think these are from trout caught on a hot day a hundred years ago, and if you're like me, that makes your mind go all soft and gooey.

.   .   .

I USED my 8½-foot 5-weight Clark most of those days on the Frying Pan—it's still my favorite fly rod—but I did break out the old San Francisco Winston for a day, and when we hiked up to some beaver ponds to catch cutthroats, I took the 7½-foot Thomas & Thomas Special Trouter.

Summers fished various Summers rods that Binder was drooling over, Ed fished a sweet old Granger Favorite, Binder fished God knows what all, and A.K. alternated between his workhorse 6-weight Clark and his magnificent prototype Heddon President—a rod he keeps talking about retiring, but that he's fished enough that it's had to be refinished twice.

There was some snazzy lumber around, but now we were really *fishing*. We all happened to be doing it with bamboo rods, but that was no longer the point. Binder said later he'd felt the gears shift that first day on the Pan when he asked A.K. if he wanted to try a certain rod, and A.K. said, "Maybe later, right now the fish are biting."

STEVE finally decided he had business to take care of (a bad bamboo rod habit takes capital to support) and Summers had a plane back to Michigan to catch, so they left first. A.K. got to thinking about all the fly orders he had to tie and left a day or two later.

Ed and I stayed on awhile longer, but the fishing was so good we were running out of things to prove, so when we came to the end of the groceries it seemed like it was probably time to go. We stopped in Basalt for breakfast before we drove our separate ways, and I got a *Rocky Mountain News* from the machine in front of the cafe, more to find out what day it was than anything else. The headline said that the invasion of Kuwait by Iraq would probably cause an increase in gas prices.

"What invasion?" I said.

"I don't know," Ed answered, "but welcome back to civilization."

I know it bothered A.K. not to be among the last to leave, but he'd finally located a pod of fish he couldn't catch, and that, after days of fabulous dry fly fishing, seemed to satisfy him somehow.

These trout were in a tight little backwater against a steep, moss-covered shale cliff miles downstream from the head of the Green Drake hatch. It was one of the prettiest and most difficult spots I've ever seen on a trout stream. The current you had to cast across was fast and too wide to reach over. The current you had to get a drift in was braided and flowing pretty quickly in the other direction. The right cast put an S curve in the line with one belly upstream in the main current and the other upstream in the opposite direction on the far side of the stream with enough snap in the delivery to pile the leader for a drag-free drift of maybe 6 inches.

The trout were big, some of the biggest we'd seen. They were rising happily to Pale Morning Duns, nosing up into the current and then dropping back, never in the same exact spot for more than a few seconds at a time.

If you've been toying with the idea of getting a bamboo fly rod, watching A.K. cast will push you over the edge. I've seen it happen. On a lawn or casting pool he looks like anyone else who's a pretty good fly caster, or only slightly better because of that fluid, almost relaxed pace bamboo trains you into. But on the water, with rising trout and conflicting currents . . . Well, it's just something you have to see.

He never did hook one of those fish, although he did miss a strike or two. He spent hours at that pool, taking a break to fish easier water only to rest it. When we first found this place, A.K. was using either the Heddon or his 7½-foot 5-weight Clark, I don't remember. When we went back the next day, he switched to the 8½-foot 6-weight Clark. You could say the spot captured his attention. He said it called for a rod with some reach and, once a fish was hooked in that fast water, some authority.

A.K. manages to have more fun than any fisherman I've ever known. Here's a guy who's fished for God knows how many years in Michigan, the Mountain West and a handful of exotic locations. He's one of the top professional fly tiers in the country, author of one of the best fly-tying books ever written and owner of a pile of fine bamboo fly rods, all of which get used.

Still, every fish he hooks might as well be his first, and every fish he can't catch is some kind of profound joke. Once in a while he'll say "Shit!" when he misses a strike, but nine times out of ten he'll laugh out loud.

That's what he did when he finally reeled in and walked away from that pool, knowing he'd be breaking camp in the morning—he laughed, said, "Well, that was fun," and wiped off his rod with a bandanna because one never puts a bamboo rod back in the case wet.

On our last day, Ed took up A.K.'s position at the pool and, after several hours of trying, caught one of those big trout. It was as simple as that, as amazing things always are when they finally happen, although catching a trout that A.K. couldn't get is not something that happens every day. It was a brown, 19 inches, Ed guessed, and he usually guesses small.

When I got home I called A.K. and told him about it.

"Good," he said, "good for Ed. What rod was he using?"

11

THE POACHER:
A FICTIONAL
FISH STORY

Harvey had done it to me again, even after I'd gone to some lengths to make sure it was on the up-and-up this time.

"Wanna get some big rainbows?" he'd asked over the phone.

"Uh, where?" I asked suspiciously.

"Private stretch of river I have access to," Harvey said matter-of-factly.

"Yeah, right."

"No, honest," he said, "this time I have permission."

"Now let me get this straight," I said. "You have spoken with the landowner. You said, 'May I fish on your river?' and he said, 'Yes, you may.' Is that what you're telling me?"

"You got it," Harvey said.

"Promise?"

"I promise. The guy's an old friend of the family. Known him for years."

"Harvey," I said, "I don't want you to get me in trouble again."

"There won't be trouble," he said. "Just bring some size 12 Elk Hair Caddis flies, a couple of Hare's Ears—same size—and maybe a few streamers. These are going to be nice, big fish." Then he hung up the phone. It had been a while, but I still knew where and when to meet him.

We did not talk about the fishing on the way to the river. Instead we talked politics, which Harvey tends to do when he has a captive audience. That is, Harvey talked (or maybe you could even say "lectured") while I mostly listened, occasionally interjecting what he might consider to be a rigorous thought. I like Harvey's political views, which is to say I don't necessarily agree with them, but they do make me want to look past the particulars and strive for a kind of clarity of my own.

For instance, on this drive the subject of conservationists in general came up because of a proposed dam project I'd been working against. It hadn't been going well. The group that had formed around the issue was loose and poorly organized, as collections of nonprofessional idealists tend to be, with most of them talking loudly about the poetry of nature and sport and a few of us—what I considered the levelheaded faction—at least trying to address the economic issues. At the moment, though, most of the collective energy was going into finding a name for the group. They wanted the initials to spell out something dramatic, like FLOOD or HAVOC.

Harvey said, "The trouble is, you guys are all whiners and dilettantes. You talk principles to unprincipled people and then wonder why you always lose. What you should do is identify the two or three politicians and/or businessmen who are most responsible for this dam going in and kill them. That would tend to elevate the discussion."

"I don't think the organization would go for that," I said.

"Organizations," Harvey said, "are, by definition, organized, and therefore both predictable and ineffective. Clear thinking and effective action emanate from a political party focused enough to have only one member."

He stopped to concentrate as the Land Rover negotiated 50 yards of especially bad road, and then continued.

"I, for example, am a Jeffersonian Zen Buddhist Agrarian Anarchist. There are few committee meetings."

At that point we pulled up to a weathered gate with a hand-painted NO TRESPASSING sign square in the middle of it. The NO had been shot out long ago with some kind of big-bore firearm.

"We're here," Harvey said. "Get the gate."

"You have the key?" I asked.

"It's not locked," he answered.

And it wasn't.

Harvey spilled the beans when we were on the river, tying dry flies to our leaders. The big trout were just beginning to boil at the surface of the water. It would be dusk in an hour and the first caddis flies were coming off. It looked like the fishing would be good, and for the next few hours it would only get better.

"If the old fart spots us at all," Harvey said, "he'll come down on the other side of the river, scream and yell, maybe fire a wild shot or two. If we have to, we can make it out before he drives the 5 miles down to the bridge and then all the way back up here."

Tall cottonwoods stood along the river there in a gallery grove. We were on the inside of an oxbow bend that formed a pool the size of a respectable beaver pond. Swallows were flashing in the air over the water, eating the caddis flies. The river wasn't all that big there, but it was too deep for a man to wade across or a truck to ford. I can't say I was completely surprised to learn that we were, in fact, poaching again.

"What if the guy calls the sheriff?" I asked.

"The sheriff will take even longer to get here, if he comes at all," Harvey said.

"Can this guy shoot?"

"Couldn't hit a barn from the inside," Harvey said. "This is entirely cool, virtually risk free."

"I don't know, man . . ." I began, at which point Harvey lost his patience.

"Look," he said, "if your poor little sensibilities are really wounded, you can hike back to the gate in about twenty minutes. From there on you'll be just another respectable citizen walking in a perfectly legal way down a Forest Service access road. I'll be along to pick you up in maybe two hours, not long after dark. You'll have been a good little boy. I'll have 10 pounds of fish. Now, if you'll excuse me, there's only so much daylight left."

Maybe I knew when Harvey parked the Land Rover behind a rock outcrop a hundred yards farther than we'd have to have been from the river. But, once I thought about it, I guess I really knew for sure back at the gate, although I don't know exactly how.

Hell, if the truth was known, I knew what was going on when he called me about this in the first place.

Harvey was wading down the bank, false casting, looking for the biggest fish within range.

"One thing," I said. "How did you know the gate would be open?"

"I came out and sawed the chain off yesterday," he said over his shoulder. "I don't know why I go to so much trouble for you."

· · ·

You see, Harvey had taken it upon himself to educate and enlighten me. I was a puss, he'd said, a slave and a coward like all the rest, but there was a faint spark of something there. If I sucked it up and showed courage, it was possible that I could be saved; possible that I could live some kind of a life.

In the beginning I'd actually sought the guy out. I started hearing about him as soon as I moved to town and it became known that I did a bit of fly-fishing.

Harvey is something of a local legend: born right here in the county; married his high school sweetheart and now has a small spread outside of town. It's the kind of marginal little ranch that looks meager and hopeless when you first drive past it, but that, on closer inspection, is actually tighter, more efficient and more expertly patched than most. The clutter is the kind that comes from work in progress rather than work abandoned. The bird dogs that trot out to greet you exude the casual air of seasoned professionals on their day off, although at first glance they just look tired and a little beat-up.

Harvey was known to run a little stock; buy, sell, trade and fix trucks and guns; do some blacksmithing and to dabble in a dozen other things, too, some specified, some not.

Here's where the stories began to conflict. Some said he'd done everything, while others said he was an accomplished liar: a forty-some-year-old man with stories that, when laid end to end, covered more than a century.

Harvey was also known to live well. Too well, some said. There were veiled hints from some quarters that he now and then dealt in controlled substances, while others claimed that he was just a hard worker and a master of the barter system.

And he was said to be a poacher and trespasser of mythical proportions, the slipperiest in five counties, a baiter of game and a dynamiter of trout, although here the stories diverged again. Some said he wasn't a poacher at all, just a local who knew everyone for 60 miles in any direction; a good, respectable hunter and fisherman who was smart enough not to reveal his spots. Others said he was just smart enough not to get caught.

Harvey was clearly slippery in one way, though: He'd lived his whole life in and around a single small town and the people there *didn't* know everything about him.

When I met him—I didn't go out of my way, this town is of the size where you meet just about everyone in the first year—he just seemed to be your regulation hippie/red neck hybrid, maybe with slightly more than his fair share of the rural crazies, but basically harmless and pleasant enough. So I asked him if he wanted to go fishing on the Franklin Ranch.

I hadn't been around here long, but I'd wangled permission to fish there by asking politely, closing all the gates behind me and by keeping a brace of trout for old Mr. Franklin and releasing all the rest. I was rather proud of this spot, and it was the best thing I had to offer.

"Sure," Harvey said. "I've fished there before, it's good."

Harvey wore coveralls, patched hip boots and a baseball cap that day, but he had a good vest and a fabulous rod: an old Thomas & Thomas 6-weight bamboo fitted with a small Hardy Perfect reel. He turned out to be a stylish caster and an all-around good fly fisherman. He fished the entire evening rise with one flawlessly tied #16 Adams dry fly, although his vest bulged with what looked like quite a few fly boxes.

The guy at the bait shop had told me Harvey's vest also contained a little Browning .380 automatic pistol that he used to return fire on any landowner who decided to pop off a warning shot for effect. But then that was also the guy who had mentioned explosives.

"As long as Du Pont keeps making dynamite," the guy had said, "that Harvey will keep catching fish."

I'd heard that kind of thing before. Sometimes it was true, mostly it was sour grapes. After that first trip to Franklin's, I figured half the talk I'd heard was just that: talk. Harvey was the local fishing source—a guy I should try to get close to—and some people were jealous of him, that's all.

Of course, when I took Mr. Franklin his two trout, the old man nodded at Harvey, who was leaning against my truck lighting a cigar, and said, "Traveling with some pretty fast company, ain't ya?" But then that could have meant anything. You know how old ranchers are.

WE took to fishing together a couple times a month that season, and Harvey showed me some fabulous spots where the trout were always at least half again bigger than what I'd been catching on my own. Now and then we'd go in on what seemed to be a more roundabout route than was necessary, sometimes we parked the car pretty far back in the trees, and I'll admit we hopped a few barbed-wire fences here and there, but I figured the guy just had connections. He was a genuine local, after all, and I was just along for the ride.

Okay, I guess I *did* have my suspicions, but no one ever challenged us, and it was going very well. There was never a crowd on the water, and we were catching some very large trout. Harvey always kept two or three big ones for supper. His wife, June, was reputed to be a wonderful game cook. They ran some cattle, as I mentioned, but they ate nothing but wild fish, game birds and venison.

"Beef is bad for you," Harvey said. "Too much cholesterol, and the animals themselves are dumb and unattractive. You are what you eat, you know."

Harvey also tended to be away a lot, usually with only the barest of explanations, like, "I was just over at Decker." June took this cheerfully in stride, leaving the impression that she alone knew where Harvey was and what he was doing and, further, that it was okay with her.

Two things should be mentioned here: First, June is quite possibly the prettiest grown woman in town; second, there are those who think she and Harvey are the perfect couple, and others who don't.

Once, at the cafe, I overheard a friend of hers ask June, relative to a recent disappearance of Harvey's, "Is he out tending his crops, or what?" referring to a widely circulated tale having to do with a booby-trapped marijuana plantation in the national forest. Then the woman added, "Why do you put up with it?" Naturally this was done in a half-earnest, half-joking tone so it could be taken either way.

June picked up the light side of it, added a cryptic smile and said, "Well, Beth, some of us just appreciate cowboys more than others."

ONCE we went to fish a lake Harvey knew about that had some big brown trout in it. Of course we went at night because large brown trout are known to be nocturnal. I couldn't even tell you where the place is now. We drove in well after sunset on a dirt road that forked many times, and we covered the last half mile or so with the headlights out. We were in the Jeep that time, and Harvey had the windshield folded down so he could see better in the darkness.

At that time Harvey owned a Jeep, the Land Rover, two pickups (one with a camper for trips, the other with an open bed for chores) and a Volkswagen Beetle. At any given time, maybe three of the five would be running.

He'd told me to bring the heaviest rod I owned rigged with a weight-forward line and a level 20-pound tippet. He'd gone through my streamer box that afternoon and picked out four of my largest Muddler Minnow streamers.

"Put these in your pocket for tonight," he said, "they're all you'll need. And bring a landing net."

Harvey, usually a pretty cool customer, seemed excited. It was catching.

That night at the lake we fished in hip boots, close to shore. There was no moon. You could see by the stars just enough to get around, but nowhere near enough to fish. We were casting blindly and feeling for strikes on the retrieve.

I caught a huge trout. It hit my streamer with a dull thump, like a snag. When I set the hook it came alive, shook its head ponderously and fought like a big fish, using almost nothing against me but its considerable weight. The fish took me fifteen minutes to land on a heavy rod.

When I got him in the net, I took out my flashlight and shined it on him. It was a brown trout, 26, maybe 27 inches long, bigger around than my thigh. The fish's back was dark, its belly was deep, it had a snarling, kyped jaw and a glazed, brutish look in its eye. The fish was way too big to be anything like pretty, but it was by far the biggest trout I'd ever caught.

"Son of a bitch!" I yelled. "Harvey! Look at this! Wow!"

Harvey materialized out of the darkness over my left shoulder. "Douse the goddamned light and be quiet," he whispered. "And kill that fish," he added. "June will bake that mother up."

So I was quiet. I made five quiet casts. I could hear the line swishing in the stillness and the plop of the big weighted streamer on the smooth surface of the lake. I heard what sounded like an owl way off in the trees, and then I heard an outboard motor. It didn't start quietly and build, it was just there as the boat came around the point in front of us.

Harvey said, "Freeze," and a big-beam flashlight shone out from the direction of the boat. I glanced over at Harvey. He was just a shape in the darkness 20 feet away. If I hadn't known he was there I might not have seen him at all. I couldn't tell for sure, but it looked like he'd dropped his rod tip in the water, put his chin on his chest and was just standing there, stock still.

I did the same.

The boat was going fast and was on us in no time flat. The guy went by a hundred yards out, playing the flashlight beam along the bank. It flickered on Harvey first and then me, and I thought, We've had it, but then the boat and the light continued down the shore toward the southeast, the sound of the motor fading, the beam playing quickly in the trees.

The guy had been looking for guilty, scared figures running through the woods, not posts standing in the water. He hadn't seen us. It was amazing.

For an instant there, when it looked like we were caught, I felt this overpowering need to be forgiven, but then that was replaced by an ecstasy of relief, and no matter how hard I tried I couldn't make the guilt come back again.

The sound of the outboard faded until I could hear the swish of Harvey's line in the air. He'd started fishing again.

So that's when I stopped going fishing with Harvey. Not because I'd finally figured out what we'd been doing, but because I'd finally gotten scared.

I put it to him on the drive home that night, as I cradled that enormous trout in my arms, the slime of it leaking through my shirt, feeling deathly cold on my chest and stomach. He should at least have the decency to tell me what was going on so I could make up my own mind, I said, adding, "Sooner or later we're gonna get caught, you know."

"Poaching," he began, "is an interesting concept. It relies on the idea that the land and the game do not belong to the people. I don't know how that notion got started."

It was a long drive back and I wish I had a transcript of all Harvey said. It would have been a revolutionary document. I remember it now in bits and snatches:

"I'm not a poacher, I'm a traditional hunter/gatherer exercising my God-given right to live off the land."

"Where is it written in stone that the game belongs to the state to portion out as they see fit?"

"It's not my job to obey the system. It's the system's job to deal with me."

"If you think you own your house, try not paying your taxes once."

"Store-bought food will eventually kill you. If not the food itself, then the ease of getting it."

"Nothing worthwhile ever came shrink-wrapped in clear plastic," and so on.

That was the night he called me a puss and a slave, which was insulting at first, but later got me to thinking long and hard about a lot of things. It was impossible for me to disagree with Harvey's premise. The wrong people *are* in charge, the system *is* steering us away from an honest, self-reliant life, store-bought food *will* eventually clog up your heart and prostate.

But I was scared of the sheriff, the landowners with flashlights and, presumably, guns, and I was a little scared of Harvey: scared of these truths he wanted to illustrate for me and of how much he seemed to like me. He had, after all, taken me under his wing. He had taken me places that he'd never taken anyone.

In the end I put the larger philosophical questions on the back burner and simply decided against a life of crime. Harvey called a few times with invitations to go get these or those big trout, and I turned him down, saying I was busy. After a while he stopped calling. We'd wave on the street, talk at the cafe, and that was that. I fished on public water, where I caught smaller fish and fewer of them.

But then he'd called with this transparent ruse about having permission, and I tumbled for it. I guess I was flattered. I thought he was going to do it by the book just once, just for me, so we could go fishing together again. If the truth was known, I like Harvey, and I sort of missed him.

And if it was a lie—as it turned out to be and as some gnawing suspicion told me it was from the beginning—then that was still flattering. He wanted to take me fishing, and maybe he thought I needed some excitement. In fact, hadn't I told him that just a week before when we ran into each other at the hardware store? He said, "Hey man, how's your life going?" And hadn't I said, "Okay, I guess. A little tame, though."

What, exactly, had I meant by that? Well, maybe nothing. Maybe that's just the kind of thing you say to Harvey.

So there I stood, trespassing on God knows whose land, vacillating between being mad at Harvey for luring me there and being pleased that he had, as he put it, gone to so much trouble for me: not only by lying, which, in my experience, Harvey doesn't do much, but also by driving out the day before to saw the chain off the gate to quiet the suspicions he knew I'd have.

That was brilliant. Mad or not, I had to hand it to him. He had planned to tell me the truth in the end (or let me find out for myself) but he wanted it to be on the river. He wanted me to see those big trout first, to stop thinking and just confront the reality of the situation, as he'd once put it.

I stood there stewing for five minutes, holding a strung-up fly rod, watching big rainbows rise to pretty, tan-colored caddis flies, and arrived at the following decision:

Figure it all out later. Right now, fish. I was there. The fish were there. I wanted them and I knew I could get them. There was a kind of refreshing immediacy to it.

We did well. The trout acted like they'd never been fished for in their lives, and in an hour we each had four 16 to 18 inchers on stringers and had released a lot of smaller ones. The sun was setting and the air had turned cool, but bats had not yet replaced the swallows over the water.

It was just dusk when the pickup truck came slamming through the trees on the far bank and skidded to a stop about 10 feet from the water. I reeled in, grabbed my stringer, and started trotting up the bank. I was almost to the trees when I heard the guy yelling. I couldn't make it all out, but I could catch pieces of it: "bastard," "thief," "jail," things like that.

Harvey hadn't moved. He was standing in knee-deep water watching this short, thin man hopping up and down on the far bank the way you'd watch a doe and a fawn coming down to drink.

Then the man reached into the cab of the truck and lifted a scope-sighted bolt-action rifle from the rack. I took another step toward the trees and glanced back at Harvey, thinking now he'd surely follow me. Instead he unzipped a pocket on his fishing vest and reached in.

The man on the far bank chambered a round and fired into

the air. He seemed to enjoy that, so he did it again. The rifle was very loud.

That seemed to satisfy him. He put the rifle back in the truck, yelled something about the sheriff, got in and drove off.

"How many fish you got?" Harvey asked, zipping up the pocket on his vest.

I had to count them. I'd forgotten.

"Four," I answered.

"Well," he said, "I guess that's enough. Let's hit it."

On the drive home Harvey discussed the relative merits of the .30-06 and the .270 for elk.

We'd been at Harvey's house for about twenty minutes, long enough for June to admire the fish and for Harvey and me to clean them. We'd just opened a couple of beers when the pickup from the river, a blue Chevy, pulled up out front, followed by a blue-and-white Blazer with a sheriff's star on the door. Harvey walked out to meet them, beer in hand. I followed, but stayed on the porch.

"This man says you two were trespassing on his land," the deputy said, nodding at the short, thin man standing beside him. Close up I could see he was maybe sixty, with sharp features and watery eyes. The rifle was hanging against the back window of the pickup cab.

"When?" Harvey asked.

"Just now!" the short man said. "Less than an hour ago, you son of a bitch!"

"Less than an hour ago I was down at the highway bridge fishing," Harvey said. "I got a limit and came home."

"Were you with anyone?" asked the deputy.

"No, I was alone," Harvey said.

The deputy looked at me and said, "You know anything about this?"

"I just came over to borrow a pair of pliers," I said.

"It was them!" the man said. He sounded hoarse and looked a little desperate. Pointing at Harvey he said, "I seen his red pickup."

That was a lie, of course. We'd been in the green Land Rover, and the way Harvey had driven in and parked behind those rocks, no one on the far side of the river could have caught even a glimpse of it.

I felt sorry for the guy. He wanted Harvey badly, and he'd seen him driving around in that old red pickup for months, as we all had until last week when it broke down.

"Well, here's the red pickup over here," Harvey said, leading both men around the side of the house where the truck was up on blocks with the transmission out and disassembled, all the parts lying on a big sheet of cardboard.

There was some more discussion, mostly between the deputy and the old man, but I couldn't hear much of it. Judging by the body language, the old man was madder than ever, wishing he'd shot us both when he had the chance, the deputy was sorry, and Harvey was getting bored.

Then the man and the deputy walked back to their vehicles, got in and drove off in different directions. Harvey knelt down on the cardboard to rub some grit off of one of the pickup's gears.

I hadn't noticed how dark it had gotten until June switched on the porch light over my head. "You'll stay for supper, won't you?" she said through the screen door. "These fish are really gonna be good."

12

MONTANA

I'VE SPENT A GOOD DEAL OF TIME in Montana over the years, but, as any of my friends from up there will tell you, I'm still a tourist from Colorado: a guy who drives up to the Big Sky Country when the fishing is good, but who spends his winters safely at home, in the balmy climate of the foothills 700-and-some road miles to the south.

They'll say "balmy" because when it's 25 below zero here—as it occasionally is—it's 50 below in Montana. Of course with the windchill factor, that would be more like minus 80. If it snows 3 feet here on the Platte River drainage, you can bet they got 10 feet in the Absaroka Mountains, or at least that's what they'll claim.

My friend James Goossen wrote from Billings last winter saying it was so cold he saw a lawyer with his hands in his own pockets.

This "ours is bigger than yours" business is the kind of thing Texans used to pull until everyone got sick of it, but in this case it *is* true for the most part. Montana is bigger, emptier and less civilized than Colorado. At last count, there were fewer people in the whole state of Montana than there are in the city of Denver (a favorite statistic of Montanans and Montana-lovers alike). Consequently, the place is richer in fish, game and open land. It's also tougher to make a living there, and, yes, the winters can be horrendous. Having spent some of my boyhood in Minnesota (which is roughly level with Montana on the map), I understand that living through bad winters is a justifiable point of pride.

There's a mythology in operation here, and most Montana writers have gotten around to authoring the "I Was There When the Big One Blew In" story; you know, the one about that first monstrous blast of winter coming in from Canada: the storm that shows us who's boss. These things usually read like notes from the edge of the world. They're all similar, and they're almost always good.

I guess I'd always been a little envious of that—it's hard not to envy those Montana writers in any event—but now, after this last trip in the final week of October, I finally qualify.

I'd been hunting with Dave Carty, and it had been one of those brilliant trips. We'd shot many Hungarian partridge over Fancy the pointer in the fields around Bozeman and Livingston—with one especially fine day almost in the foothills of the Crazy Mountains—then we'd gone up along the Madison River with Poke the springer to get some ruffed grouse out of the places where the aspen and spruce came together.

(Yes, it probably goes without saying that the upland bird hunting in Montana is better than it is in Colorado.)

And then, flushed with sport and intrigued by variety, we headed up to the country around Denton, where Dave said we might be able to get into a few pheasants.

The pheasant cover was mostly along the Judith River, and Dave had permission to hunt on a ranch up there. There were also some Hungarian partridge on some local farms that, of course, Dave also had access to. We were in Dave's pickup camper with provisions, spare clothes, guns, maps and both dogs. The camper is a little oversized for the truck, so it wobbles from side to side like a Gypsy wagon.

We drove up from Bozeman and went to the wheat field first, just to get a few birds to start this leg of the trip off right. This was the place where Dave said he'd had his best Hun hunting that season. The weather was cool, crisp and bright: good for walking, but Dave said he wished it was wetter. Fancy doesn't scent the birds as well when it's dry.

No more than twenty steps into the field we jumped a small covey of partridge. They flushed in front of the dog rather than holding for the point, and they were well out of range.

We followed the birds for an hour or so, flushing them out of range and then chasing them down again until they started to get tired. This is strenuous work, and later Dave told me I'd held up well. He used to live in Colorado himself, but he's been in Montana long enough now to have taken on some of the native characteristics. What he meant was, I'd done okay for a guy from the banana belt of the Rocky Mountains. He'd have expected even less of me if I'd been from, say, New Jersey.

Dave was surprised that the birds were so spooky. In an accusatory tone, he suggested that maybe the farmer was letting someone else hunt on his land. Dave has many widely scattered places to hunt. That way the shooting is more natural, and, although he kills a lot of birds, he never takes too many from a single covey.

Finally the birds flushed over a low rise, and when we came over the top, a single got up. I missed it. We found that the birds had split up into singles that got up one at a time. Dave says this is standard practice for quail, but unusual for Huns.

We worked the field carefully, and Fancy did well. Dave shot two birds, I shot one.

While all this was going on, a breeze had come up, and it was a cold, steady one: the kind of autumn wind that cancels out the warmth of the light and then makes the sun itself seem chilly. I thought it was blowing out of the northwest, but I couldn't be sure. Back home the mountains are orderly and lie north to south. Up there the ranges are scattered all over the place, so I can't always tell where I am. From the high spot in that field I knew you could see the Judith Mountains, the Little Belt Mountains and the Big Snowys, but I couldn't tell which was which without the map.

I could have asked Dave, but didn't. For one thing, it didn't much matter. The pertinent bit of information here was that a big front was coming in quickly—any idiot could see that. For another, no true outdoorsman wants to have to turn to the guy next to him, point vaguely toward a distant cloud bank and ask, "Uh, is that north?"

As we worked those single birds with the dog, the breeze turned to an outright wind with moisture in it. The temperature dropped and there were visible slivers of snow in the air half an hour before the bank of smooth, charcoal gray clouds finally turned the sky dark. Disoriented or not, I could tell this was the kind of storm that comes from the north, down out of Canada. I did recall from the map that there was no range of mountains between us and the Canadian border, and at a time like this, "Canada" forms up in the mind as a dusty stubble field between you and the Arctic Circle.

We headed back to the camper for more clothes and wool hats. A blow like this can mean the end of it for a while, so we weren't anxious to stop hunting, even though exposed skin was beginning to sting.

Poke was locked up in his kennel. He whimpered joyfully because he thought we'd come back to get him, then he cried pitifully when he saw that we hadn't. Out there on that open, windy dirt road, he sounded pretty goddamned mournful.

We decided on one last, quick swing, and the last covey got up out of range again, with the wind, and were gone like missiles. The air was thick with snow then, and we couldn't see where they went. I remember thinking that, in the hand, a Hungarian partridge is a fat little bird covered with great fly-tying material that does not look very aerodynamic. Without much discussion we groped our way back to the truck and lurched off through the snow in what Dave said he thought was the general direction of Denton.

You know Denton: it's out in the middle of the open hay fields along the Judith. This is hunting rather than fishing country, although that, I suppose, is an out-of-stater's perspective. I've actually been told that there are plenty of trout in the streams out there for those who know when and how to fish them, it's just not the "high-fashion razzle-dazzle you tourists are looking for."

Anyway, Denton: It's about 7 miles up the county road from Coffee Break. There's a two-block, mostly one-story main street, much of which was clearly built before World War II. The same goes for most of the houses, of which there aren't many. This is an eminently practical town where you don't blow a lot of time and money building new stuff as long as the old stuff is still serviceable. There's no fly shop and whatever basic items a guy might need in the way of sporting goods can be picked up at the hardware store. Naturally, the tallest building is the grain elevator.

We had supper at the cafe (chicken-fried steak with gravy, canned vegetables, homemade rolls) and then parked the camper along the railroad tracks out by the grain elevator. This is the kind of informal industrial park that is technically private, but that's far enough out of everyone's way that you can probably camp for the night undisturbed. The local policeman may rattle your door at three in the morning because the camper isn't a familiar one, but he may not make you move, especially in a snowstorm.

It was stinging cold by then, with snow falling steadily in a high wind, and ten minutes into the settling-in process we learned that the camper's heater didn't work, even though, Dave assured me, it had worked fine just two weeks ago. After finding and studying the directions and then attempting a field repair, we lit the burners on the propane stove to take some of the chill off. It was better than nothing.

We slept that night with one burner turned to low and a couple of vents open for fresh air. The camper rocked like a boat in the wind, and snow rasped on the windward side. The small windows got milky with ice inside and out. Luckily Dave had brought both dogs, so we didn't have to fight over who got to sleep with a warm puppy. I got Poke, the temperamental genius who snores.

We'd had a few beers that evening, so naturally I had to get up in the middle of the night to relieve myself. I was barefoot and I wasn't thinking, so when I stepped outside the bottoms of my feet stuck to the steel tailgate of the truck like a wet tongue to a pump handle. I could picture being found just after dawn, half naked, frozen solid in an undignified pose. I began to empathize with cattle that freeze in their pastures on nights like this. There would be a moment of enormous helplessness, during which you would go ahead and pee anyway—one last, completely practical act before death set in. But then my feet began to come loose and it appeared that I would live through the night after all.

I had just enough of my wits about me to glance over at the town. Nothing moved and no lights were on. It's quite possible that many doors were unlocked. I could easily see from one end of it to the other through the snow. The geometric lines of the buildings were softened by the shapes of cottonwood trees in the yards, and it looked no more out of place on the northern prairie than a collection of magpie nests.

.   .   .

BY six the next morning the wind had calmed and the air was cold enough to freeze my breath in my beard when I peeked outside. The sky was still low and gray, but it had stopped snowing. Smoke was coming from some chimneys, and plumes of exhaust marked a few pickups that were warming up.

We decided to bundle up and hunt, but when we found that the truck's engine wouldn't turn over we figured we'd better walk into town for a strategy session over coffee and pancakes. The dogs, assuming we were leaving them to starve and freeze, whined horribly. Hunting dogs who aren't hunting are pretty miserable anyway, and for some reason they always think the worst of you when things get a little grim.

We hiked over to the same joint where we'd had supper. It had been pretty good and it also seemed to be the only cafe in town. A dozen trucks were parked in front of the place, but otherwise the main street was empty.

We'd no sooner sat down and ordered breakfast than an old feller at the counter said, with an air of unquestionable authority, "Two degrees this morning." A dozen large men in coveralls and baseball caps nodded silently over their coffee. Either this guy was always right, or they'd all looked at their own thermometers. Every thermometer in town would have come from the hardware store across the street, so there'd be very little variation between them. It was 2 degrees out, no doubt about that.

Then the man said, looking at us, "You boys are hunting." Native Montanans don't inflect much, so a question sounds like a statement.

"Yes," I said, "birds."

"I was here before these birds was," the old man said, gazing out through the frosty window as if he could still see it like it used to be. Presumably the skyline of Denton would have been about the same back then. I thought of asking, "You mean these birds in particular, or the species?" but I knew what he meant and it's probably best not to be a smart ass with someone you don't know.

Turns out he didn't much care for the Huns or the pheasants ("chinks") because they were both introduced species and he thought they'd gotten together and run off most of the sharp-tailed grouse ("prairie chickens," locally). He knew we weren't after the chickens because that season was closed.

Of the grouse he said, "I used to shoot five a day behind where the bank is now." After a sip of coffee he added, "I was here before the bank, too."

The bank itself looked none too new. It was the kind of place that might once have been knocked off by armed men in fedoras driving touring cars.

The first newspaper I'd seen in a week was a thin one from Great Falls. It said that the presidential campaign was as nasty as ever, but that the whales trapped in the ice off Alaska had been saved. The cafe was warm and steamy enough that the newspaper was limp.

On the way back to the truck we stopped at some kind of machine shop with an OPEN sign in the window and asked a total stranger if we could get a jump. "Sure," the guy said, "take my car. The keys are in it. Cables in the trunk." There was only the one car.

Later I would have time to be amazed that this guy would just give his car to a pair of scruffy-looking hunters he'd never seen before—that kind of thing really doesn't happen much back home—but at the time it didn't seem too unusual.

I never did figure out what kind of shop it was, and I didn't give it a lot of thought because we were off to start the vehicle, chip the frozen dog water dish from the floor of the camper, and find some pheasants. There was no sign on the place, but I guess everyone in town already knew what it was, so they didn't need one. Denton is the kind of place where you don't make a big deal out of what should be obvious.

As it turned out, we would not get skunked that day. Dave would bag a couple of partridge in a stretch of sagebrush where we didn't expect to find them. When they flushed, I stood there marveling that the birds were in that kind of cover, while Dave, working on instinct, executed a nice double. Eventually, I made a nice shot on a high-speed cotton-tail. We would only see three cock pheasants in range: Dave missed one out along the river, and the other two were in a front yard in Denton, right next to some dead flowers in a white-painted tractor tire.

It was all winding down anyway. The following day I would get on a plane in Bozeman and fly back to Colorado. I had a bunch of frozen birds in my luggage—insulated with dirty laundry; I had staked out two small, obscure trout streams to try next summer; and I had been there when the Big One blew in. To tell you the truth, it was no bigger than the ones we have back home.

13

A YEAR
IN THE
LIFE

A FEW NIGHTS AGO, FEBRUARY 13 to be exact, A.K. and I were driving back from our third trip this month to the South Platte River. It had been a cold, breezy day on the water, so when we finally broke down the fly rods and pulled off our waders, it felt good to get out of the wind and warm up in the cab of A.K.'s pickup. Say what you like about big, old American trucks, they have seats like couches and great heaters.

It felt so good, in fact, that as we drove up the canyon to where we catch the highway at the town of Pine, we began to get a little drowsy from the combination of warmth and weariness. This called for coffee and maybe a Snickers bar, but we didn't stop at the first little store, because by dark on most days the coffee there has turned lukewarm and sour. Instead we went 10 miles on down the road to the place where the coffee would be more or less fresh and where I could put real milk in mine instead of that white, powdered stuff. Being traditional field sportsmen, we understand these intricacies of survival.

The conversation picked up after that, and we began to congratulate ourselves on how close we'd come to hitting it the way we wanted to. February is when the good midge hatches usually start on the Platte. That's the *good* ones, as opposed to the thin, spotty ones that may or may not come off through midwinter. Around here, February usually has the first real dry fly fishing of the year.

The midges aren't as predictable as the Blue-winged Olive mayflies that come on in late March or April, but the expectation is definitely there. You can hit a decent midge hatch in December or January, but you'll consider it a tremendous break, while the same thing in February—though it's only slightly less rare—seems only right.

On each of the two previous trips down there we'd found a few trout feeding sporadically on the surface for a short time in the afternoons. Not what you'd call a proper rise, but, still, a handful of fish coming to the surface to eat little bugs with wings on them—a clue that the real hatch was building up. We'd caught most of our few trout those days on nymphs, but A.K., through persistence, had managed to hook a few on dry flies. Nymph fishing is okay—its saving grace being that it's difficult—but when you're doing it while waiting for a hatch to start it can begin to drag a little.

This last time—from about noon on—the trout had been nosing up into the faster water at the heads of the pools, feeding on midge pupae, and every time the wind would go down for a few minutes, they'd rise to the surface.

It was the wind that finally did it to us. It wasn't quite too strong for fly casting, but it ruffled the water enough that the trout couldn't see the size 24 midge flies on the surface, either ours or the real ones.

How many variables are there to hitting good dry fly fishing in the off season? Dozens at least, from great astronomical considerations down to the moods, currents and wind riffles in a stretch of river no larger than a bathtub. To guess only one thing wrong is a sort of victory. We'd caught a few fish as it was, but if it had been a calm day, we'd have hammered them. Or, so as not to sound too confident, we'd have had the opportunity to hammer them. Catching big, smart trout on tiny flies and 7x tippets in low, clear, cold water is not what you could call a foregone conclusion.

We planned the next trip for the following week, Wednesday or Thursday, when the front that caused today's wind was past and the next one would be somewhere between approaching and settled in.

Like all fly fishermen, we hate wind, but we also know that when you're trying to fish the hatches you have to court it. The best dry fly fishing seems to be on gray, wet, clammy days when the barometer is either low or dropping. You want it calm for all kinds of reasons—so you can see the rises, so the fish can see the bugs on the surface, so casting is easier, so you don't die from the windchill—but you also know the proper weather is the kind that *makes* wind.

Perfection in weather is hard to come by here in the Rocky Mountains, but the perfect days do materialize; days when a slow-moving or even a rare stationary low pressure system sets up over the river and, for a few precious hours, doesn't blow or clear but just squats there, dark, cold and drizzly. Eventually you come to believe in the old fishermen's weather mythology, because days like that are always good.

You can never really count on them, but you know they'll happen if, as A.K. says, you go out often enough, always carry a rain slicker and learn to cast in the wind.

After enough trout fishing you develop a specialized perspective that some see as gloomy. On a bright, bluebird afternoon in April, someone will say, "Isn't it a nice day?" and you'll answer, "Humph."

So we talked and drove and sipped coffee and, somewhere around the Turkey Creek turnoff, A.K. made the annual announcement. "Well," he said, "I guess the fishing season has started."

Since you can fish legally all year here in Colorado, the beginning of the season is a personal matter, and figuring out when it is means you've learned something fundamental about how (and maybe even why) you fish. A.K. and I fish together for a lot of reasons, but mainly because we've arrived at this kind of thing together and now agree that the fishing season begins at that instant when catching trout on dry flies becomes more likely than unlikely.

This usually happens in February, but it's not a date you can mark on a calendar. It slides around from year to year. Still, when one of us declares the season open, the other no longer feels moved to point out that it never closed or that we've actually been fishing off and on for a couple of months.

It's just communication between friends, which, with time, evolves into a form of shorthand. If we're on the stream one afternoon and A.K. says to me, "It'll get darker sooner the longer we wait," I'm likely to say, "Yeah, I see what you mean."

So, although it's possible to fish hard right through the middle of winter, A.K. and I usually settle on going out a few times in late November, December and January to catch some fish as a kind of observance of the fact that it can be done. Usually we fish with fly rods in what open water there is, sometimes we noodle some trout or perch through holes in the ice, but mostly we take what amounts to a little less than three months off. A.K. ties flies for sale, I tie some flies for my own use and write. We go out when there's a break in the weather and/or when the shack nasties get too bad.

But there's something resembling a work ethic in sport, and when you decide the season has begun, things change.

If you miss the midge hatch in December or January, you recall the times when you hit it in the past, agree it was just nice to get out, and pretty much bag it. The season is on when you spend the drive home talking about *why* you didn't hit it this time and, more to the point, how conditions could shape up better in the next couple of days.

Your work habits begin to suffer, and you go down to the store to buy a big box of plastic bags and six cans of dolphin-free tuna because suddenly you're making a lot of sandwiches.

There was a time when former wives and some friends would start rolling their eyes at this point, but I've noticed that, over the years, city folk with no poetry in their souls have largely dropped out of my life of their own accord, so now there is little or no eye rolling to deal with. It's just fishing season. The most natural thing in the world.

ANOTHER thing that happens is, you begin to look ahead meaningfully rather than theoretically. When I say I tie flies through the winter, I mean I do it casually until about mid-February, all the while telling myself I really should get it in gear because the season is coming sooner than it seems. That's usually just enough tying to get me geared up for the minute #20 through #26 midges I suddenly realize I don't have enough of.

Naturally the little flies are the hardest, so the casual practice time is crucial. A.K. doesn't experience this—being a professional fly tier and all—but if you take a few months off from tying and fishing, your fingers turn to hams at about the same rate the wading muscles in your legs go soft.

A.K. has several midge patterns of his own design that work well for him and his customers. I end up copying a lot of what A.K. does—and I have been known to use his patterns—but my favorite midge is still the good old Kimball's Emerger. A.K. doesn't like this fly because it's ugly. I either think it's handsome enough or I like it precisely *because* it's ugly, but it catches fish anyway. Something like that.

This is a hackleless fly pattern, but I tried adding a sparse hackle to it this year to make it float better and land upright more dependably. A.K. thought that was a good idea when I told him about it. "It might make the thing a little prettier," he said.

That comment almost stopped me. When you get into fixing things that aren't broke, you can run afoul of the Law of Unforeseen Consequences. After all, I thought, tying hackle on a fly that works well enough without it might be like putting flying buttresses on an outhouse.

So I tied a half dozen with hackle that I'll try on the next hatch. If they don't work, I'll give them away and forget about it. If they do work, I'll tie a few more in different sizes and colors, but I won't throw the hackleless versions away, because they *have* worked and will again when the occasion arises.

That's why we carry so many flies: so that when what should work doesn't we have plans B through, say, E to resort to rather than just giving up. You *will* give up from time to time through the season, but it should always be by choice—because you're tired, or you've already caught enough fish, or you've been fairly beaten. You should avoid having to give up because there's nothing left to try.

ALL fly fishers carry as many patterns as they can, but we dry fly fishers are the worst. For one thing, our fly boxes don't reflect what you could call the reality of the sport, that is, that trout do the vast majority of their feeding under the surface on nymphs, larvae, pupae, crustaceans and other yucky-looking forms of aquatic life. If practicality was the issue, a guy would carry boxes and boxes of nymphs and a few well-chosen dry flies for the odd hatch.

But we dry fly types do it the other way around. We carry five or six boxes of floating patterns—those pretty, clear plastic boxes with the pool-table green felt bottoms—and maybe one old blue plastic case full of nymphs.

Bill Kelly, aka "Catskill Bill," a fisherman from Sullivan County, New York, calls dry fly fishers "10 percenters," based on the premise that trout do only 10 percent of their feeding on floating flies. I don't know exactly where that figure came from, but it's widely accepted and I like it well enough that I may start using it as a motto. I don't know if they still do it, but back in the 1960s, members of the Hell's Angels started proudly wearing "1%" patches after someone said in print that it was only one percent of the bikers that gave the rest a bad name.

Ten percent actually seems about right when you think about it; an appropriately slim chance for success in a sport like this. Fly-fishing in America still has a rural, Protestant flavor to it, and most of us live with the ideas that failure is the natural outcome of any human endeavor and that anything that's too easy isn't as good for the soul as it could be.

I T'S only February, but we're already talking about what happens after we hit the midge hatch on the Platte. The probability that we *won't* hit it seems low. We'll just keep driving down there. Fishing season is on.

After the midges should come the early Blue-winged Olives. Probably the little #22s first, and then the #18s, with that almost inevitable day when the midges will hatch in the morning and the Olives will come off in the afternoon. If we take a long shore lunch complete with a fire and coffee, we could spend a whole day without ever defiling our leaders with lead weights and sinking flies.

We'll try to hit this early on the Platte and maybe a little later over on the Frying Pan, a trip that will involve the first tent camp of the year. If the Olives run long enough on the Pan, we might try to combine that with what Roy Palm calls the Mother's Day Caddis Hatch on the Roaring Fork. This is a hatch we've never seen, but Roy knows it well and he has a boat.

Somewhere in there we'll doubtless hear from some frantic fisherman that the stoneflies are on somewhere—probably the Fork or the Colorado—and we'll probably go at least once and just miss it. A year wouldn't seem complete without blowing at least one stonefly hatch.

From then on the dry fly fishing should pick up. There will be little early brown stoneflies, followed by little yellow stoneflies, with the many species of caddis beginning to emerge as the weather warms.

Midges will hold on in some of the tailwater rivers, and they'll be important throughout the whole short high-country lake season. Some of those lakes will also produce great hatches and spinner falls of Callibaetis mayflies—Speckled Duns and Speckled Spinners—although there's no telling when that'll happen. There are about sixty good mountain trout lakes in the national forest, wilderness area and national park that form our home range, and the only thing you can be sure of is that sometime between the first week in July and the middle of September the Speckled Duns will hatch on about half of them.

There will be the little Pale Morning Dun mayflies in there somewhere—at different times on different rivers— plus the tiny Trike duns and spinners, various species of mayfly lumped together as Red Quills, a #14 yellow mayfly locally called a Sulpher (although I'm told eastern fly fishers would disagree with that) and, of course, the Green Drakes.

You can pretty much plan on the Green Drake hatch on the Frying Pan, where I've seen it last as long as six or even eight weeks. It's less predictable and shorter on the Roaring Fork and maddeningly sporadic on some smaller streams I know of. On some of the creeks you'll find them in two sizes, not unlike the Blue-winged Olives. The entomologists say it's the *Ephemerella grandis* and the *E. flavilinia,* but I prefer to think of them as the #10 and the #14.

Late in the Pan hatch there's a darker bug that some call a color phase of the regular Green Drake, others call a Slate-wing Drake or a Great Red Quill, and that a few snoots insist on calling an *Ephemerella coloradensis.* Some years ago A.K. and I spent a long time trying to figure out what this bug was before we realized we didn't really care. All you have to do is tie a handful of your Drakes in a sort of negative mode: a reddish body with a green rib instead of a greenish olive body with a reddish brown rib.

After the Drake hatch on the Frying Pan and some other rivers, the hatches will come full circle and you get the late Blue-winged Olives and midges. It's almost like early spring again. Even the weather is about the same.

LAST year we had one of our best week on the Frying Pan, the kind of trip a dry fly fisher just has to talk about.

The river was supposedly in a slump that summer, after getting famous in previous years for its artificially inflated trout. It seems the Division of Wildlife had planted some deep-dwelling freshwater shrimp in Ruedi Reservoir to feed the lake trout. This was a species of little crustaceans that lived at such dark depths they were clear. No body color at all.

But Ruedi is a bottom-draw dam—which accounts for the great tailwater fishery in the river below it—and the shrimp began to peter out into the stream. Naturally, the trout ate them, and in a few seasons the upper river was full of huge rainbows so fat and ugly they were almost obscene.

Just as naturally, fly fishermen came from all over to catch these things, local fly tiers went half mad trying to tie a clear scud pattern, and, from the point of view of those of us who have fished there for a long time, things generally went to hell for a while.

But then the scuds finally all flushed out of the dam, and one year the enormous, ugly trout were just gone. Word got out among the yuppies that the Frying Pan was in the shit hole, and they all blasted off for the next hog factory on the agenda.

Panic had set in, although all that had really happened was the Pan was pretty much its old self again: a beautiful little river with its usual astonishing dry fly hatches and lots of pretty, healthy, normal-looking trout. There weren't as many 20-inch-plus fish as there once were, but the accepted local wisdom was that, now that those nasty old hogs were out of there, the younger fish would fill in that slot in a season or two.

We were there in that week when July turns into August and the Green Drake hatch is still below the catch-and-release stretch up under the dam. There were some fishermen working the hatch, but not too many, and they all tended to cluster at the advancing head of it, so we'd just fall in behind this small mob and have all kinds of water to ourselves.

We would have figured that out for ourselves eventually, but we didn't have to. That first day I'd asked Roy down at the Frying Pan Anglers shop in Basalt where the Drakes were coming off. He said to look for a bunch of guides and sports and then fish a mile downstream. "The sport is the guy fishing," Roy said. "The guide is the one in the fluorescent hat standing next to him, pointing at the water."

In the afternoons, just as the Drakes were beginning to thin out, the Pale Morning Duns would come on. The fly that worked was a thing Roy and A.K. designed and that A.K. ties for the shop. It's like a Ginger Quill, except the wings are lighter, the hackle is yellower and there's a subtle pinkish color to the quill body. Roy calls it a Frying Pan Special.

Many of the fishermen on the river have now taken to calling Pale Morning Duns "PMDs," which I don't like because it reduces poetry to a set of initials and leaves the impression that these guys are in too much of a hurry to wrap their mouths around a pretty, Old World phrase. I guess it's better than the scientific terminology, though. Now and then you'll still meet one of those bug men who see you examining a natural fly and wade over wearing the dour expression of a fly fisherman about to speak Latin.

We fished for days. I forget how many, but no one wanted it to end. Every night in camp we congratulated ourselves for staying on the old water while the fickle headhunters had moved on, and wondered if this could last into next season.

We were catching trout every day, lots of them, and all on dry flies. There were as many as five of us fishing together at times, but we never felt crowded and I don't think anyone ever tied on a nymph. When the dry flies weren't on, we just didn't fish. Consequently, the camp was neater than usual.

For my caddis flies, I usually try to tie Elk Hair, spent, low water and skittering versions in dark and pale colors, all of which I could get in a single box if it wasn't for the giant lake caddis patterns that take up so much room. For the small stoneflies I use something that closely resembles the Len Wright Skittering Caddis fly.

For small mayflies I try for regular hackled flies, parachutes, thorax ties and no-hackles, often in both dubbed body and quill body versions. The Callibaetis dun can be copied nicely with either the A.K. Best Olive Dun Quill or the standard Blue-winged Olive (not to mention the good old Adams) in sizes 14 and 16, but I like to tie a special pattern with mottled gray partridge wings to mimic the speckled wings of the naturals.

The bigger mayflies usually pass with collar-hackled and parachute styles, although that apparent lack of confusion is usually made up for with color variations.

The midge selection is built around the Kimball's Emerger, with various trailing-husk and winged, hackled flies in different colors and sizes from 20 to 26.

Mayfly spinners are dubbed-body and quill-body flies with whole feather, clipped hackle or poly wings. A Red Quill Spinner in the right size could pass for just about any spent mayfly, but I like to have Chocolate, Ginger Quill, Pale Morning Dun, Callibaetis and tiny black and white spinners, too.

Then there are the Royal Wulffs, plus some buoyant-as-cork Royal Humpies and a couple of other white-winged flies for fast water, and the Adams dry in sizes 12 through 20— just because pure imitation isn't always the answer.

I'm not a real nut for terrestrials, but I like to have some black and cinnamon ants, flying ants, beetles, grasshoppers and crickets. Sometimes—rarely—there are actual falls of terrestrial bugs, but mostly they're good search patterns to work in the dead times between the morning and evening hatches in summer. This is when most fishermen will fish nymphs in the deep water, but A.K. and I feel that terrestrial dry flies are *fished,* while nymphs are usually *resorted to.*

We both carry emerger patterns to cover some of the mayfly hatches, and we have more or less worked out the touchy matter of definition here. That is, a dry fly not only floats on the surface of the water, it also has wings of some kind. Hackle is preferred, but technically optional. If it floats but doesn't have wings, it's a greased nymph.

We settled on this to put an end to those long theological discussions that would ensue if I caught eight trout on a floating nymph and A.K. landed six on a righteous dry fly.

The way it stands now, he would have done better than I did, number of trout notwithstanding. And if we're in the same situation and I put split shot on my leader and dredge up a hog brown from deep water, A.K. will be sympathetic. "It's a great fish," he'll say. "Too bad you didn't catch it properly."

This extends into the fly tying as well. We try to tie good-looking nymphs with the right materials, but when it comes right down to it, the wing case and shell back on a dark stone nymph can be any old feather dyed black, while the wing on a dry cricket really should be natural crow—black, yes, but with those subtle, purple, wasplike undertones.

Where this idealism comes from I can't exactly say, especially since we do fish nymphs and wet flies when that's what it takes and, for that matter, one of my favorite flies of all time is the Hare's Ear Soft Hackle, an ancient wet fly pattern that, as near as I can tell, harks back to the days when most fishermen thought of a dry fly as one you couldn't get to sink right.

There have been days when we just walked around during the dead times, dry flies tied to our leaders, looking for the odd rising trout in a backwater and waiting for the hatch to come off, but just as often we fish nymphs when that's all there is to do, and we do it more or less happily.

I guess what I'm saying is, we consider ourselves to be dry fly purists, but if you watched us fish on any given day, you might not be able to tell. It's more along the lines of an interior landscape.

I T's also interesting that the dry fly ethic applies to trout and maybe grayling in flowing water, that it's less important on lakes and ponds, and that for other species of fish it dissolves altogether.

Maybe it's because we've both been at this for quite a while now, and started back when artfulness still outweighed practicality. The winged insects trout rise to—and the flies tied to imitate them—*are* lovely for the most part. Mayflies look like sailboats or angels; midges are delicate; caddis flies are quick and almost mechanical and crane flies look like miniature flying bicycles. The giant stoneflies are horrible up close, but in the air they look like armored hummingbirds. The underwater stages of these insects, however, all look like either worms or cockroaches.

It could be as simple as that: prettiness, plus the smaller

chance of success that makes this a sport in the first place. Or maybe we just read too many of those old books where the authors said they'd rather fish chicken guts off a dock than tie on a wet fly, or words to that effect. We were young and impressionable once, you know.

And I think this thing we have for bamboo fly rods has something to do with it, too. It seems a shame to use a fine, handmade casting tool to lob a weighted, short-line nymph rig 10 feet when you could do the same thing just as well with a broomstick.

That might be why streamers are a kind of sidebar to all this—almost a separate discipline. Streamers sink, but you still *cast* them.

I guess we'd be hopeless snobs if it wasn't for that work ethic I mentioned. You fish as if how you go about it matters deeply, but you can't forget that it matters for unimportant reasons. It's not like religion. You're not trying to be saved through good works, nor are you looking to bring down the infidels. There's nothing like logic to this; nothing you could use in an argument and no reason to argue except for fun. It's just something we like to do: a habit, like wiping your hands on your pants.

I was fishing the Platte River with Ed once when a nymph fisherman waded past and said to him, "I guess you're gonna fish dry flies whether the trout want 'em or not, huh," and Ed said that was about the size of it. End of debate.

It seems to me that dry fly fishing is a lot like writing. There's room for great artfulness (not to mention the constant danger of self-indulgence), but in the end it's usually best when it's hard nosed: Start at the beginning, say what you have to say, and stop when you come to the end. The paragraph that begins "And so, as the sun sinks slowly in the west . . ." should always be deleted. There are even deadlines. A good mayfly hatch will probably only last a couple of hours, so you do the best you can in the time you have.

I ran that analogy past A.K. one day on a river somewhere. We hadn't seen a rise for hours and we were just standing around talking and waiting for the hatch to start. He said it sounded good, but he thought I was spending too much time thinking. "Maybe you should tie on a nymph and catch a couple of fish," he said.

14

EVEN
BROOK TROUT
GET THE BLUES

FISHING IS A COLLECTION of instants: moments when it either comes together with amazing perfection or goes horribly wrong. Never mind the vast silences between those times when something actually happens. Sure, the long, dead times set the tone, but you usually forget about them even as they're happening, or file them under some broad heading like "dues paid."

The hours of driving or hiking and then not catching fish once you're there are like the blank paper in Taoist paintings meant to suggest fog, out of which comes a single tree and half a bridge made more poignant by all that empty space.

Or maybe fishing is more like poetry: a different, more organic way of putting things together—very likely a superior way—that goes light on rules. There's really only one supreme rule in fishing. Namely, don't get too sappy about it or people will think you're a cream puff.

WHEN it's all said and done, I think brook trout are my favorite fish, if only because good ones are so unlikely out here in the West—"good" meaning "big," of course, the complicated philosophy of aesthetics notwithstanding.

Brookies were originally introduced into the Rocky Mountains back around the turn of the century on the premise that more fish would naturally be better than fewer fish. That seemed reasonable at the time, but it turned out that brook trout outcompeted our native cutthroats for food and spawning habitat, and some biologists now trace the decline of many cutthroat fisheries to the introduction of brookies. In some places brook trout have been poisoned out so cutthroats could be reintroduced.

Brook trout also have very loose spawning requirements, so they tend to overpopulate, stretch the food supply and become stunted, sort of like bluegills in a pond with no bass to eat up most of the little ones. The fact that brookies seldom live past four years also helps keep them small, and it doesn't help that they're now mostly found in the backcountry where life for a trout is hard anyway.

The introduction of brook trout here is now seen by some fish culturists as a classic example of doing the right thing in the wrong way, a good-hearted mistake.

In his definitive *Standard Fishing Encyclopedia,* Al McClane says brook trout do fine in their native range— roughly from Georgia to the Arctic Circle and as far west as

Michigan—but in general they do not introduce well. And, he goes on, "Large brook trout occur in the same regions where they existed millions of years ago—with very few exceptions."

Naturally, it's those few exceptions that interest fishermen most.

Brookies have an odd, contradictory status with western fly fishermen. We like them, but we think of them as little, which puts them in a whole different category. They're fun, they're pretty, but no one wants to hang a stuffed 8-inch fish over the mantel, or brag that he could have, but he turned it loose. Even the name "brookie" is diminutive.

We also tend to consider them easy, so we can't even agonize over fly patterns like we do—and want to do—when we're engaged in the more profound business of stalking big trout. If you hold to the full mythology of the sport, brookies and bluegills are the only two fish you can legitimately expect to catch on poorly tied #10 Taiwanese McGintys from K mart.

But we do like them because they fill a need. In fact, they may actually embody the complete aesthetic of the sport: Fly fishermen have an investment in being serious while at the same time not actually taking it all seriously, so we like these little fish precisely because they're little and easy, even though as a rule we're into trout that are large and difficult.

However, because they're usually small, a big one is noticeably more mythological than a big rainbow, brown or cutthroat, so when a brook trout reaches a certain size we can get more excited, walk farther, stay out later and tie more flies than we did when we were just being serious. See?

AROUND here, the rare large brook trout occasionally comes from water where it doesn't belong—out of nowhere, in other words. You'll go into a bait shop or marina at a big reservoir and there on the wall, among all the huge stuffed rainbows, browns, pike and lake trout, will be a 3- or

4-pound brookie on a plaque. It'll be half to a quarter the size of any of the other fish, but big for a brook trout—well worth mounting.

Oddly enough, it doesn't look small by comparison, but stands out as something even more outrageous than the 20-pound Mackinaw right next to it. Maybe it's just the broad orange stripe at the belly, green back, white fin margins, yellow spots mixed with red dots haloed in blue. Brook trout are gorgeous, and taxidermists paint them up like neon signs.

This fish was caught accidently by a troller, or maybe by a kid casting spinners off the bank for stocked rainbows. Whoever hooked it, it was probably the last thing he expected.

Brookies themselves are seldom stocked anymore, so how this one got in there is a mystery. The standard explanation is that it was born high up in a feeder creek, washed down in the spring runoff, somehow escaped being eaten by the big fish in the reservoir and then spent its short life growing to great size.

Or maybe there really is a small population of them hanging on in there from the old days. That would be plausible, since the big, shallow, fishy western reservoirs are something like the lakes in the brook trout's home range, where some of the really big ones come from. There's lots of room, lots of food and lots of big, predatory fish to keep their numbers in check, so the relatively few that survive can grow large.

You'll hear other theories, but the upshot is always the same: It's a fluke. There may be a few more, but it's not like you can expect to catch them. Big brookies are the exact opposite of the eager, easy little ones. As they become great, they tend to sink from sight.

SEVERAL years ago, Jay Allman and I were fishing some spring-fed prairie ponds in southern Wyoming, where the trout were gigantic. These were perfect stock tanks: secluded, private, water chemistry like champagne, forests of weeds, vast herds of bugs. No way they could have been any better. The ponds were full of rainbows that ran from a fat 18 or 20 inches on up to fish we couldn't land on good, stout tackle under favorable conditions.

But in the pond we spent the most time on there was supposed to be this giant brook trout. That is to say, Jay said he'd caught it once, either earlier that year or the season before, I don't remember which. He said it had come from the little inlet arm, that it had taken a leech pattern and that it weighed around 7 pounds.

He'd released it, so it was *supposed* to still be in there— even bigger now, you automatically think. Just the one, as far as he knew. Why and how? Who knew. Washed down out of the Medicine Bows one spring, or dumped in by one of the men who shared the lease, or dropped by a clumsy osprey. Who cares?

There's a significant difference between the big trout story and the actual report, but when the guy in the next float tube caught the fish and can point to the spot, you'd have to be the ultimate cynic not to buy it.

We never caught the fish or even saw it, but several times a day one or the other of us would paddle slowly up to that little inlet and fish it with the fly that was currently working. Not a fresh fly, but a used one all gooed up with rainbow slime so it wouldn't smell of human.

One can only wonder about some of the hogs we lost. They were almost certainly big bows because they fought that way—the few seconds of throbbing when you set the hook, the fast run that could backspool a reel with the drag set too light, then the not quite audible "ping" as the leader broke— but you can't be sure. I have no idea how a 7-pound brookie fights, and when it's between one kind of trout and another, guessing what you had on that then broke off is like calling a coin toss and then losing the quarter.

I don't know about Jay, but I caught more sheer tonnage of trout in a few days on that pond than I would land over the rest of the season. They were all rainbows, but I remember the place now as the little spring pond where there's supposed to be a big brook trout. Sure, it could have died of old age by now, or been caught and kept by someone else, but no fisherman ever really believes that.

IT was the same story when Gary LaFontaine and I fished on the Blackfeet Indian Reservation in northern Montana five or six years ago. Rich prairie lakes, big rainbows and rumors of leviathan brook trout.

"Where?" we'd say, and we'd get a different lake from everyone we asked, not to mention a different weight—8, 9, 12 pounds. There weren't many of them, though, everyone agreed on that.

That was the trip where it rained constantly. It was early in the year, cold, bitter, and the harder it rained, the better the fishing got. We didn't catch a lot of trout, but it seemed like each one was bigger than the last. But no brook trout, not even little ones. Maybe we were on the right lakes and maybe we weren't. There was no way to tell.

One day we stopped at a hardware store in Browning. To make conversation, I asked the guy behind the counter how long it was going to keep raining. He said he didn't know, but the old man on the front porch could tell us.

So we asked. What the hell. The old man looked at the sky, held up one hand with the fingers spread and said, "It gonna rain five days."

It did, of course, but he could have heard that on the radio.

Out here, at least, that's how it is with big brook trout. They're supposed to be there, but you don't catch them, and you finally pack up and leave with the feeling that something unusual has happened.

BROOK trout sometimes crop up in the work of certain observant writers whose books have "trees in them," as Stephen Bodio says. I like to think this is a bit of literary resonance that's missed by readers who know only that a brookie is a kind of fish.

In Jim Harrison's novella *Brown Dog,* his main character says, of Michigan and, incidentally, of fishermen, "There is something in the air up here that makes us lie a lot. For instance, if you catch three brook trout you say you caught fifteen, and if you caught fifteen you say you caught three."

That's exactly how I am with beaver ponds. There's a moment in the life of the right beaver pond—a moment that lasts maybe a season or two—when it will have big brook trout in it.

You start with a small, Spartan stream up in the mountains. It holds a few brook trout, but the conditions are marginal, so the fish seldom get very big. A 9 or 10 incher is a whopper, and there aren't very many of them. For that matter, there may not be a whole lot of fish total—large or small—and, considering the brookie's tendency to overpopulate, that shows you how tough things are.

But when a family of beavers erects a new dam, the neighborhood improves overnight. There's deep water for cover and protection from winterkill, more insect habitat and a spike of nutrients from all the flooded vegetation. The few brookies lucky enough to find themselves in there have it wired, and they'll grow relatively large.

I'm told that in flatter parts of the country beaver ponds can be large enough to float a canoe and they can last a long time, but out here they're usually small and have short life spans. After a few spring floods they may silt in, and in a really good flood the dam may blow out. In my experience the overpopulation business begins to kick in about the time the habitat has begun to degrade, and the whole thing can happen in as little as five or six seasons, with the fourth or fifth summer producing the biggest brook trout. By the time a beaver pond appears on the latest USGS map, the big trout are probably gone. You can miss it, but if you manage to see it, it's a little like watching geology happen.

Seizing the moment on beaver ponds means a lot of walking and exploring. You need to check known beaver meadows for new ponds every few years and try to remember what you found so you can come back at the right time. You also have to make a guess at where the pond is in the process.

A brand-new dam with green sticks in it and a few little trout in the pond can mean a wait of three or four seasons, which can strain the memory down the road. "Okay, was that two years ago now, or three? And, come to think of it, which creek was that?" All of a sudden the mountains, which you'd begun to think were getting a little crowded with tourists, seem vast and trackless again.

I don't do it, but a guy should probably keep a journal on this, complete with map references. You never make notes on the map itself because people might *see* your maps. As it is, I spend a lot of time catching little fish, and I find it's possible to lose my concentration, ending up with the gnawing suspicion that up one of several little mountain creeks there's a beaver pond that should be about ready. Naturally, this means more walking, but if I start to worry about my memory, I can console myself by thinking, Well, at least I can still hike.

I feel I understand the process, but I tend to scout beaver ponds when I'm in the right mood, or when the fishing elsewhere is poor, or, rarely, when the fishing is so good I feel I can take a break and walk up some little creek just to see what's there. I do understand it, but when I find a hot beaver pond, the best I can call it is informed luck.

And if I catch fifteen big fish I say I caught three little ones.

I've seen the same kind of cycle happen in mountain lakes, although here it's less predictable and not even guaranteed to come off at all. A few years ago I was grouse hunting with James Goossen and his Lab Max the Wonder Dog. As so often happens, we'd walked many miles and found no grouse. It was a cold October day; calm, with a light snow falling. I decided we should go look at a nearby lake because I was losing heart and because the moment you give up without actually going home is often precisely when you find birds.

This was a small, rugged lake near timberline that was known to have some little brookies in it. I hadn't fished it in several years and didn't know anyone who had. When you find a lake full of 6- to 8-inch brookies, you tend to write it off. I'd have come back to check it out if they'd been baby cutthroats, but little brook trout don't instill much faith.

The lake was slate gray and dead calm, so we could see the rises from a good distance. Even from a couple hundred yards the fish looked pretty good, and up close the boils were impressive. It can be hard to accurately tell fish size from the rises, but you could see these weren't tiny trout.

James asked Max not to get in the lake, and we walked down the bank trying to get the dull light at an angle that would let us see into the water. The fish were feeding on a good midge hatch and some of them were wallowing close to the surface, with their dorsals and tails showing. It was still hard to tell their exact size—you need a fish in the hand for that—but I guessed them at around a foot long with a few pushing 14 or 15 inches. There weren't many fish, just a small pod of them feeding along the east bank.

I couldn't actually see that they were brook trout, and I suppose the Division of Wildlife could have dumped some cutthroats in there. Still, there were brookies a few years ago, and if the lake had been restocked I'd probably have heard about it. Clearly a working theory was needed.

All I could figure was that the lake had winter-killed a few seasons ago, pruning off most of the fish and leaving a few survivors with more than their usual share of food and room, starting a fresh cycle at some indeterminate point in the past. I'm told that can happen.

But "why" wasn't the problem. The problem was, there were good fish rising, but it was late in the year for high lake fishing. Already there was a skin of ice on the shady side of the lake. This could well be the last hatch until spring. It was late in the afternoon—about time to start heading back—I was standing there with a double-barreled shotgun and the nearest fly rod was 30 miles away, most of it on bad roads. I really wanted to see one of those fish, and it struck me that some of the closest ones were just about in range.

It was one of those irretrievable moments, and I asked James, in what I hoped was a casual tone of voice, "Do you think Max would retrieve a trout if I shot one? Hypothetically, that is."

"Hard to say," James said suspiciously, adding, "And I'm pretty sure that's illegal."

Right. If it wasn't illegal it should have been, so I decided against it. I'd gone for many years without shooting a trout, and I guess I wasn't ready to start.

In the grand scheme of things, those weren't big brookies, they were "good ones." Still, around here a 14- to 16-inch brook trout is about the best you can expect, and even then you're pushing the limits of probability, so I'd have to say they were big enough. I've caught a handful of 16-inch brook trout hereabouts—at least half of them in a private pond A.K. and I were invited to fish last fall—and I watched Mike Clark take an honest, measured 20-inch brookie through the ice from a lake where, the summer before, I'd taken a single 17 incher.

These are all exceptions, which explains all the whooping and yelling and snapping of photographs.

If you want to really "get into" big brookies, as they say, your best bet would be to fly up to the Hudson-Ungava Bay region of Labrador, one of those places McClane was talking about where big brookies have existed for millions of years and, by all accounts, still do.

Or maybe you'd try the Nipigon River in Ontario where the world record brookie (14 pounds 8 ounces) was caught.

That happened way back in 1916, but the fishing is still supposed to be great.

I talked to a guy who'd been up there once. He usually has a lot to say about fishing, but when I asked him if it was worth going he said, "Yes."

Are the brook trout as big as they say?

"Yes."

When a normally talkative fisherman changes his tone like that, something intense is in the works. Maybe it was so good the poor guy was still stunned six years later.

I may yet go up there because there's part of me that thinks the big brook trout should be at the end of a long journey into the fish's home range, culminating in a trip in a single-engine plane with pontoons and then maybe in a wooden boat poled by an Indian guide. In a way it would only be right: back to the source and all that.

I've done things like that before and they've usually worked out well. The fishing wasn't always as easy as I thought it would be, but it was dependable. The big ones were in there, the guide at least had a clue and sooner or later you'd probably get one. Maybe even a couple.

I've now and then wondered if the safari is an adventurous, stand-up way to attack the problem, or the dilettante's way out of many long walks and fishless days. I've never made up my mind on that, so I guess I'll have to keep trying it both ways. One thing I *have* learned is that failure is harder or easier to swallow depending on what you have invested: three thousand dollars, or five bucks worth of gas and a cheese sandwich.

Then there's another part of me that thinks the big one should come from my own backyard if that's humanly possible. After all, a 20-inch brook trout in Colorado would be the fish of a lifetime. It was for Mike, and it would have been for me, too—even through the ice on a hand line. But if I went to Labrador with half a dozen fly rods and *didn't* catch 20 inchers, I'd have to fight the idea that it was a bum trip.

In fishing there's a fine line between the impossible and the merely unlikely, the point being to reach as far as you can without actually losing your grip. I know there are a handful of monster brook trout in Colorado, and I also know the best way to catch one is to take up trolling for Mackinaws in the mountain reservoirs and hope for the best.

But, although there are no clear rules, these things should be gone about properly or not at all, and when you're thinking in terms of small waters and a bamboo fly rod, it's a different game. When you're looking for something that might be there but probably isn't, the practical edge is off and you know you're on a more philosophical errand.

When A.K. and I go out for brookies we usually figure 9 inches is good enough, measured from the tip of the thumb to the tip of the little finger with your hand spread as wide as it will go. Usually we release these and anything else we catch, but if there are a lot of them and we decide on a trout dinner, four fish of that size will just fit in my square cast-iron frying pan.

I guess I've accepted A.K.'s view of brook trout from his days in Michigan, where they're native and also the official state fish. There the brookie is the backwoodsman's trout: maybe not big, but wild, pretty, dependable and good enough to eat to make up for the size.

And they're seen as easy, *in a way*. That is, put a reasonable fly in front of one of these fish and he'll probably take. Okay, but the best ones live in creeks flowing under impenetrable willow tunnels in remote, boggy, bug-infested, quicksandy swamps. Whenever you talk about brook trout, there always seems to be a "yes, but . . ." in there somewhere.

Apparently, the Rocky Mountains are steeper, but otherwise easier to walk than much of Michigan. A.K. tells me overgrown western beaver meadows are nothing compared to Michigan cedar swamps, but he allows the former are still plenty hard to get around in; and large brookies are about as rare here as in Michigan.

Sure, there could be a big one—if that wasn't in the back of your mind somewhere you might not even go—but there probably isn't. Mostly we think in terms of exercise and scenery. Sometimes you have to walk a long way to get to the lakes and streams where brook trout live, and those places are always quiet and pretty.

We use bamboo rods, but sometimes not our very best ones because it's possible to fall, and that's how you break a tip. Then again, great rods are meant to be used, so the choice can be agonizing. Something like a 7½-foot 4-weight is about right because it will let small fish show off well. And if it happens to be somewhat old and maybe have silk wraps, so much the better.

We may cut the fly selection back to a box of drys and a few nymphs, leaving room in the vest for sandwiches, canteen and rain jacket, but we use the good flies, no seconds. A.K., who won't fish with a fly he hasn't tied himself, will tell you he doesn't *have* any seconds.

The fine tackle is part of it for us. For one thing, it helps us prop up the idea that we're a class act, you know, sportsmen of such stature that we can walk a long way and slog through lots of underbrush without caring that the trout aren't big. Of course we go to that trouble because the odd brookie *is* big, but it takes sensitive men like us to appreciate the delicacy of that paradox.

WE have found some good brook trout out in those beaver meadows, sometimes in a big, new pond on the main stream, but just as often hidden in some surprising little corner. There'll be a deep slot in an old side channel with the soil held in place by aspen roots, and just enough current and food to grow a decent fish.

Or maybe it's a shady plunge pool holding out below an all

but wrecked old dam where you hear falling water to your right when you know the stream is on the left. That is, it's on your left now. Beaver meadows seep and change and move around inside themselves, so what you hear is a remnant of what was the main channel maybe ten or fifteen years ago.

A nice-sized brook trout in a place like that constitutes one of those quintessential fishing moments. Here's a fish that isn't supposed to be there in the first place and isn't supposed to get big, but things have gotten right and stayed that way for just long enough, and here you come following the sound of water in what might be that trout's last season.

This will be a tough spot, so you might not be able to catch the fish. If you do manage it, you'll probably release him because he seemed happy in there, or let's just say he was exactly as he should have been, given the conditions. I don't think trout actually get happy the way we do. Whatever, you don't want to be the one to bring this to an end unless the moment has clearly lasted too long.

That can happen. A.K. once caught a 16-inch brook trout from the last deep corner of what had once been a big, sprawling pond. We were working up the creek looking for new dams and this was a place I wouldn't have bothered to cast to, but A.K. has a way of sniffing these things out.

When I saw the bow in his rod and the splash of the fish, I trotted over with the camera, but before A.K. even landed the trout we could see it was old and weak and skinny. It was an honest 16 inches—we measured it—but a third of its length and most of its girth was a big, hook-jawed head. The body was so thin you could see its ribs. The fish may not have actually been dying at that very moment, but its future sure looked bleak. The pond had gotten too small and there just wasn't enough food.

A.K. killed it, not so much to eat—although he did that and said it was good—but to put it out of its misery.

We could have felt bad about this, but we didn't. It was just mortality, pure and simple, and I think that's one of the reasons why we like to wander around in the mountains with expensive fly rods: to get a taste of things the way they really are, minus the usual crap. You'll hear people say that birth is a miracle and death is a tragedy, but a sportsman eventually comes to see that anything that happens every day is just plain ordinary. Life is just life, and even brook trout get the blues. The trick is to not get too bent out of shape about it.

A.K. strung the skinny old fish on a willow stick, held it up proudly and said, "This is why we measure 'em in inches instead of pounds."

15

PIKE

NORTHERN PIKE FISHING IS SOMETHING that gets hold of me when things start seeming too normal. There's a whole esoteric universe of pike fishing, complete with famous Norwegian pike anglers and often-told apocryphal stories, but to a fly fisherman with the usual thing for trout, it's a kind of sporting backwater, which is the kind of thing I need.

I think I fish, in part, because it's an antisocial, bohemian business that, when gone about properly, puts you forever outside the mainstream culture without actually landing you in an institution. It's a nice position. No one considers you to be dangerous, but very little is expected of you.

Okay, fine, but then you wake up one morning to find that three-quarters of your friends are also trout fishermen and they don't think you're strange at all. For instance, whatever odd thing I may have once done on a trout stream, you can be sure Koke Winter did something even odder back in 1958. When you're up against masters, you can't win.

So I go pike fishing because they're a wonderful sport fish, because I remember them fondly from childhood, because there's a whole new mythology to learn, but probably *really* because A.K., Koke and a bunch of other people don't understand what I see in it.

That's not to say I'm any good as a pike fisherman. Every time I try it again I get a fish or two and learn a little bit more about it, but as it stands now I feel as though I'm catching pike like a tourist, that is, based on good advice, but still largely by accident. I know that's a poor substitute for real skill. Skill in fishing is a nebulous thing based largely on seasoned intuition, perhaps informed by a little knowledge, but catching a few fish now and then doesn't mean you have it.

I'D been building up to pike this year because I'd completely missed last season almost without noticing. I was too busy with trout, bass and panfish in the spring, and then with trout and hunting in the fall—the two times of year when the pike fishing is best. But Ed Engle and I talked about it off and on over the winter, and when he called to say the pike were biting at a big lake we know of, I was ready.

Psychologically ready, that is, jazzed on early spring and prepared to turn last winter's talk into some kind of action. I never actually pack until I get the frantic phone call that says Ed, or someone he knows down there, has caught pike or seen them moving or has favorably interpreted some string of natural omens or has just caught a case of what Ed calls "the boogies."

Ed is a great partner on expeditions like this because he's a tenacious researcher. It seems that pike fishing has begun to catch on with some Colorado fly fishers. It's happened quietly, behind the scenes, and there's no danger that pike will replace trout as the coolest possible fish, but now it's to the point where there are accepted fly patterns, standard ways of rigging leaders and so on. Ed had sniffed this stuff out and he fed it to me over the phone, piece by piece.

When he and I first tried pike fishing with a fly rod years ago, all we knew was that we needed big flies and pretty stout tackle, something to let us mimic what we once did with plugs and level-wind bait-casting rigs. So we used our bass rods and some oversized trout streamers, the kind of setup we'd seen in articles about trolling for landlocked salmon. As trout purists, we applied the usual chauvinism: They eat minnows, so you use some old minnow imitation. They're northern pike, how smart could they be?

This worked well to a degree. That is, we caught some fish, but not any more than the trout fishermen on the same water were catching by accident, which was naturally unacceptable, even though we had a few small fish to show. We kept some that Ed's wife, Monica, turned into pike amandine. The fish's stomachs were full of crawdads, which shot the minnow theory all to hell.

Pike are delicious, by the way, and eating them is not something you'll get much grief about. Even the pike fishers believe that in the waters where these fish live there are plenty of them, and although your typical fly fisherman may not understand the attraction, he'll congratulate you on your stringer of pike because he thinks they're nasty, trout-eating vermin.

There's a case for that. I once spoke to the fisheries biologist who first brought northern pike to Colorado back in the 1950s. They were used to clean the rough fish out of some cool-water lakes but, like terrorist bombs, they couldn't be aimed. At one reservoir they ate all the suckers one year, all the dace the next and finished off the trout in the third season.

"Pike will eat anything," the biologist said, "they're great."

This season was the one where Ed decided to get serious about it—and when Ed gets serious, something memorable usually happens—so I happily went along for the ride. Being guided through something by an old friend is nearly as good as learning it for yourself.

The day we arrived at the reservoir, the wind was blowing hard and there were whitecaps on the water. Trout fishers don't like it like this, but it's supposed to be good for pike. The standard theory on this is that the wave action stirs up the insects and crustaceans on the bottom, which are fed upon by little fish, which are, in turn, eaten by big, hungry pike.

Northern pike spawn in the shallows in the spring, and then later, with the spawn over and the water still cool, they'll feed close to shore. They're a cool-water fish, though, so they'll typically retreat to deeper water during the summer. Then, in the fall, they'll move into the shallows again where a fly caster can get at them.

The most commonly used pike rig involves a heavy fly rod—a long 8- or 9-weight—and a 50-pound-test monofilament shock tippet in front of whatever you want the actual breaking strength of your leader to be. This is a saltwater-style rig that's seldom seen, or needed, on fresh water. You can land a big pike on a lighter leader, but the pike's sharp teeth are less likely to cut the 50 pound. Some fly fishermen even use wire leaders, but those are awful to cast.

At the terminal end of the leader you tie in a small metal snap. This serves two purposes: It allows the fly to work a little more naturally in the water, and it saves you from having to tie improved clinches in that fat, stiff mono or, worse yet, learn a new knot.

The most popular patterns for pike are what are called

"Bunny Flies." A typical Bunny Fly is tied on a large, salt-water hook, usually with big, bead chain eyes to add a little weight. A long tail of dyed rabbit fur (on the skin) is tied on, and ahead of that another strip of fur is wrapped on the hook shank Palmer hackle—style.

Yes, they are very quick and easy to tie. And, no, they don't quite qualify as bait, if only because the rabbit skin is tanned.

The most effective colors seem to be all black, black and red, and red and yellow. You can actually buy these things in some fly shops now, which wasn't the case just a few years ago, when pike fly fishers were apparently on their own.

The fishing itself is rather simple. You want extensive shallows with a nearby drop-off, and you want to cast into the chop, which naturally means casting into the wind. You wade out into thigh- to waist-deep water and stroll slowly down the bank, casting as you go. At least that's what you do if you don't have some other idea.

To a trout fisherman who's been trained to read water, identify bugs and strategize constantly, it seems way too random. The fish are cruising and so are the fishermen. Sooner or later one may bump into the other, although in my experience, you're about as likely to step on a pike as you are to hook one.

Still, I'm told this cast-and-walk thing is standard proce-dure on the large, dish-shaped, largely structureless western reservoirs where, at best, you may have some vague clue, such as that the west side of the lake is better than the east. There are those who are a little more attuned to the subtleties of the sport, but I am not among them.

So you walk and cast into the wind. Now and then you stop and stretch your casting arm, which is getting sore. Casting a big fly on a heavy rod into a moderate gale is not something your muscles get used to out here.

. . .

Eᴅ told me which turnout to head for. He'd been here a few times before this season and he felt he knew where the spot was. As we drove around the shore, I was surprised at how few people there were. This was a time of year when trout could be caught, although it was far from the best time, and the bright, windy weather was wrong. It was the height of the pike fishing, however, but even at that there were only half a dozen other fishermen on the whole, enormous body of water.

This kind of fishing is getting a little more popular, as I said, but there are still very few fly rod pike specialists around. One of them was clearly out there on the water, though. We couldn't tell which of the tiny wading dots in the distance he was, but we could spot his car. It was a clean, late-model four-wheel-drive wagon with a Colorado vanity plate on it that read ᴇsox. I didn't know what it meant, but Ed, with his science background, told me the Latin name for northern pike was *Esox lucius.*

I've been told you can no longer get vanity plates that say anything even vaguely resembling ᴛʀout, ʙᴀss, ꜰʟʏʀod, or anything else that obvious, because they've all long since been taken. But I'll bet this guy had no trouble with ᴇsox, except that down at the license bureau, where they try not to let you sneak by with something dirty, someone may have wondered if maybe this was Lithuanian slang for oral sex or some such thing.

Ed and I rigged up on the open tailgate. We were a little sheltered from the wind, but I still had to chase a sock across the road before I could get into my waders. Walking down to the water, the lines slapped our rods. Remember, wind is good, I thought.

I had tied some all-black bunny flies because I already had the black rabbit and figured the color couldn't make that much difference, but Ed suggested I try one of his red-and-yellow ones. He said that with the clear water and strong sun, the bright fly would probably be better. And anyway, the last few times this was the fly that had produced the best.

"We haven't really hammered them yet," he said, "but we have gotten some."

I envied him for the insight, as I tend to envy any fisherman who seems to know what he's doing.

We waded into the water then, about two long casts apart, and started slowly down the bank, heading roughly west. The bottom slopes gently here, so from waist-deep water you could cast out toward the middle of the lake on one side and back toward shore on the other. They say neither direction is regularly better than the other, but on days like this when the waves are rolling in well, the big pike often lurk closer to shore than you'd imagine.

There was also the possibility of a trout. They're in this lake, and pike fly fishers sometimes catch stupendously big ones by accident. For that matter, the trout fishers now and then inadvertently hang a pike when they're fishing something big enough, like a #2 Wooly Bugger, for browns, but even a medium-sized northern will often snap the leader smartly.

A trout fanatic I know said that's just as well, since many of his colleagues aren't into pike and don't know what to do with one when they get it. One poor innocent even tried to hand land one by its lower lip like you would a bass. He was rushed the 60 miles or so to the nearest emergency room to get sewed up, ruining a day of fishing for the poor guy who had to drive him.

There is a mythology to pike fishing, much of which has to do with bleeding wounds on dumb fishermen.

We fished down the bank together. Ed was ahead of me, so I was casting to water he'd already worked, but that didn't matter. If they were there, the fish would be cruising and hunting, so it was just as likely that one would move in behind Ed as that he'd get to them first.

We worked down this bank for, I'd guess, two hours.

The waves I was standing in seemed high. Their troughs would drop down below my butt and their crests would sometimes ship over the tops of my chest waders. One would roll through gracefully and lift the weight off my feet. Then the next would come and slap me hard. Balance had to be paid attention to. I felt like I was being shoved around.

I'd have been wet from spray, except that the wind we were facing into was cool, dry and dehydrating. The sun was bright, but it felt cool, too, or at the most lukewarm. I began to feel like I was drying out. My skin felt papery, my mouth chalky. I had a canteen in my day pack, but getting it out would involve wading to shore, and this is a persistent kind of fishing where you think twice about breaking your rhythm.

And I guess there was the suspicion that, since I had no clear idea what I was doing, maybe a little hardship would turn my luck. Wasn't it John McDonald who pointed out that the whole concept that fishing should be fun is a fairly new idea? So suffer a little. I don't really believe it, the evidence is against it, but maybe there's an intelligence out here that will take pity on me. You know, give me a fish just for having faith.

This is probably where religion came from in the first place. I can picture someone back in prehistory up against a difficult practical problem thinking, There must be something out there to help me if only because I need help so badly. In the heat of the moment, it wouldn't seem unreasonable.

I began to cast automatically while watching a mountain range to the west. In that dry, clean, windy air it seemed like it was right there, an easy hike away, or no more than a fifteen-minute drive, but I knew that it was behind—way behind—that hospital emergency room that was 60 miles off.

My mind had begun to wander. When the fishing is like this I begin to think, not cogitate or ponder, just think, about, you know, things. A day or two after I got back from this trip Susan asked me, casually, "Do you ever think about me when you're fishing?"

"Sure," I said. This is the correct answer, true or not, although it just happens to *be* true in this case.

"I don't mean just when you're out, but when you're actually fishing."

"Absolutely," I said.

AND so this is how it goes. You wade down the bank, casting. Eventually the pickup is a yellow dot back on the horizon, at which point you turn around and fish back. Then, after a cup of coffee and a candy bar, you start again at the same place, heading off in the same direction because this is supposed to be the good bank, and because it could all have changed. While you were peeling your Snickers bar, the wolf pack of big pike could have moved in. You'd never know the way you might with trout. There'd be no dainty rises speckling the surface, no lazy tailing, even if the water was still enough for you to see such things.

If you were in the wrong mood you could begin to see this as drudgery, but in the right mood it's more like a cross between meditation and casting practice. This fishing is slow, so you can't stay keyed up. You have to trust your reflexes to set up on the occasional strike.

I got a bump hours into it, that live jerk that can't be bottom or a wave or anything but a fish. My reflexes seemed to work. That is, without having to think about it I hauled on the rod to set the hook, so when the fish turned out not to be on, it couldn't have been my fault. Right?

The lake seemed enormous, oceanic. It even smelled like an ocean; not the salt, but the decomposition, the rafts of rotting vegetation washed up on shore and the inevitable dead fish the gulls and ravens pick at. I'm used to small water—creeks, rivers, farm ponds, little mountain trout lakes. This thing was measured in miles. I knew it to be full of fish, but in two or three hours I had come upon one willing pike. I was hungry and, now that I thought about it, a little tired. It occurred to me that nothing in life vanishes as irretrievably as a lost fish.

The pike may in fact have moved in, because it wasn't long

after that that Ed got a good take. I heard him say something—one of those single-syllable exclamations fishermen use, not quite a word, but a little more than a grunt—and when I looked up, he was setting the hook. He set it hard three or four times to make sure. Since not much was happening, I waded over to watch.

At first there was just weight and throbbing on the rod; that preliminary phase where the fish begins to figure out that he's having some kind of difficulty and the fisherman tries to determine how excited he should be.

The pike made a halfhearted run out into deep water, taking some line, and then Ed reeled it back in without much of a fight. This could have been a modest fish, or a hog that just hadn't gotten cranked up yet. Sometimes a big fish will seem more annoyed than anything. If you're lucky, he won't panic until he's gotten a little tired out and it's too late.

There was another run, and then Ed brought the fish back a bit closer than he had the first time. When Ed saw it, he took a step back and said, in a perfectly level, conversational tone, "It's a mother." Ed seems a little bit excited most of the time, but when there's reason to be excited, he tends to become calm.

Ed fought the fish for a while, and I figured it was a pretty good one because he was being more careful than usual, but otherwise it was hard to tell. When I finally saw the pike, my first thought was to get out of the water. It looked like a green log, and when it bored off on another run the flick of its tail threw water 2 feet in the air.

The fish is still in the water and you're not the one playing it, so the realization comes upon you slowly. No telling just how big it is, but big. Oh boy, you think, don't freak out. Don't start yelling instructions, you know it doesn't help.

You like to have an audience when a huge fish is landed, but in this case I think we were both glad no one was around. There are some odd mechanical aspects to this kind of fishing. The well-equipped pike fisher carries a gaff, long-handled hook disgorgers, jaw spreaders and a short, weighted club that a gangster would call a sap, but that a fisherman calls a priest. Unhooking a big pike is a little like changing the spark plugs in the truck with the motor running.

Ed had some pike tools, but neither of us was very experienced at this, and the fish honestly scared the hell out of both of us. A pike is a fabulously ugly fish. The body is a kind of military green, snaky but, on a big one, also obscenely fat, like a python that's just eaten. The mouth is like a leather duck bill with many teeth, the eyes are nasty and hooded, and, once you get hold of it, the fish turns out to be chillingly slimy, with clear goo looping off of it like snot.

Bluegills are precious, trout pretty, bass handsome, but a pike is in an entirely different class. You have to love them not in spite of the fact that they're hideous, but because of it.

Ed did a workmanlike job of gaffing the thing, but then, after looking around to make sure no one was watching, we dragged it up on the beach and beat it to death with a rock. We didn't want to have to touch it until we knew it was dead.

It taped out at 40 inches. Around here, any pike over 30 is considered trophy size.

We decided we had to know what it weighed, so we dragged the thing up to the truck and drove to Chaparral Park Mobile Fishing Tackle, a combination trailer park, grocery store and fishing shop that had the closest scale. Dave and Barb were happy to weigh the fish. It went 18.7 pounds on a registered scale. One hell of a nice pike, they both said.

Then Dave got out a Polaroid and took Ed's picture, or, rather, a picture of the fish incidentally being held by Ed. There's a difference. This they tacked on the wall along with maybe a hundred other snapshots of people holding fish. Although Ed's pike was one of the largest there, it still seemed to shrink amidst all those other little color photos.

There was fresh coffee on, good, strong, free fisherman's coffee that took two spoons of powdered nondairy creamer without changing color. Barb began mopping the pike slime off the linoleum floor, and Dave said, "Yeah, a guy could slip in that and break his fuckin' neck." The excitement had subsided.

Then we went fishing again, and as we got back into the grinding pace of it, the big fish began to fade for me, except for the knowledge that a big fish had been caught, which could mean . . . Well, you know.

I began to see that no great epiphany was at hand for me, although this would all go on file, and maybe someday my personal pike lore would build up to where I could look at some big, featureless bowl of stored irrigation water and think, Yes, this looks right, probably without entirely understanding what looks right *about* it.

Not too much later I did hook a pike. It was just as it should be. The fish thumped the fly hard, I set up, and he bored off slowly, but with great deliberation. I knew he was no 40 inches, but he was going to be a good enough fish. I played him into knee-deep water and hand landed him gingerly, grabbing him behind the head, careful not to get into the sharp gill covers. A good fish, but not big enough to require the gaff.

He measured 27 inches, which is a nice-sounding number to a trout fisher, although it's only a fair-sized pike, especially in light of Ed's earlier performance.

Ed admired my fish. "Good one," he said. "Healthy, pretty, nice size, and," he added, alluding to Ernest Hemingway as he sometimes does, "it showed courage."

Okay, fine, the guy who caught the enormous fish does have one wisecrack coming, and I could see that Ed deserved the big one. He'd done his homework, he'd come up here several times before to scout it out and he'd even bought a gaff and a jaw spreader. It made the kind of sense you'd expect to see if there was some justice in the world. I guess I hated him for it.

16

THE NEW POND

ONE THING YOU'LL NOTICE about fishermen is that—in the time-honored tradition of humans everywhere—they never seem to be able to get enough. Once an angler has become serious about the sport (and "serious" is the word that's used) he'll never again own enough tackle or have enough time to use it. And his nonangling friends and family may never again entirely recognize him, either.

The same thing goes for places to fish. We all say the good fishing waters are fewer now because of development, irrigation, pollution and/or excessive angling pressure. That's absolutely true, but, by the same token, there are still so many good places to fish that if a guy in, say, his mid-thirties was to quit his job and start right now, he couldn't hit them all before his legs gave out.

I've met a couple of people who actually *are* trying to hit them all, or at least come as close as possible. They seem deliriously happy one day and a little despondent the next—pretty much like the rest of us, except with better tans.

If you can afford to be a jet-setter, you'll fish in all the famous, fashionable places with the best tackle and the canniest guides, and the exceptionally hip will have fished these spots for at least a year before they were splashed all over the magazines. If you're more blue collar, you'll have a network of good local spots (many of which you'll keep quiet about) and you may put together the trip of a lifetime once or twice each season. Either way, you'll never quite be satisfied.

And that goes for the tools of the trade as well. Once something clicks and you have become a fisherman, you'll likely embark on the search for the perfect rod—which, naturally, must be fitted with the perfect reel, upon which must be spooled the perfect line. If you ever achieve that in graphite, you'll immediately begin wondering why some people prefer split bamboo.

At some point you'll probably begin tying your own flies because it's cheaper in the long run and because the ones in the stores, though often close, just aren't quite as good as they could be.

Whatever you start with—bass and panfish, trout and grayling—you'll eventually begin wondering about other fish. Maybe salt water will beckon if there's time, although there may not *be* time.

A friend will call with an unusual plan of some kind. He'll say, "I don't know if you'd be interested, but—" and you'll interrupt, saying, "If it swims, I'm at least curious."

So you diversify, learning, in the process, that the perfect pike rod is not necessarily the perfect bass rod, and so it goes. Eventually this can become what looks like a life's work.

I don't see this as greed or fanaticism. I prefer to think of it as just a healthy sense of adventure, complete with all the profound notions that can go along with that: intellectual curiosity, the role of humans in the environment, life, death, sport, gourmet food, peace of mind, whatever. Fishing is a silent, often solitary business. You're bound to start thinking.

So when a guy says something apparently harmless like, "Look, you're worried? You're hassled? You're fighting with your friends? Go fishing," he may already have begun to radicalize your consciousness. You go out there and try to insinuate yourself into the natural scheme of things by fooling a couple of fish, and the first thing you learn is just how far you get by being pushy and impatient.

You can study, upgrade your gear, carry more flies and try to achieve greater finesse overall, but it only begins to work when you finally slow your pace and take things as they come, which may be right now, in a day or so or, rarely, never.

Aha! you think.

Back home you may begin to see that human activity is the only thing in nature that doesn't seem to happen in its own sweet time, which is the real reason you have more fun fishing than you do working. You'll probably become something of an environmentalist—possibly even a radical one—although in other areas of life you may be able to take things a little easier now.

Aha! again.

This perspective on things can change you irreparably. If it comes to you early enough in life, it can save you from ever becoming what they call "normal."

When I was a boy, a kid who would rather fish than play football or speed in a car was a dork. Now he's considered a dweeb—roughly the same thing. It's a burden at the time, but it's possible that said kid will grow into one of those rare adults who can distinguish between the things in life that can be controlled and those that can't; who can perceive mistakes as natural phenomena and who can just generally remain calm: a person who, if pressed, will tell you that the universe may or may not have meaning, but it sure seems to have a sense of humor.

This is, I believe, a profitable, comforting and accurate worldview that, among other things, makes you want to spend a lot of time fishing, not, as Robert Traver pointed out, because it's so important, but because everything else we do is equally *un*important.

As I said, this is profound, but only if that's the way you want it to be. In other words, the guy who says he fishes because it chills him out and because he just likes, say, trout, is not necessarily wrong or dull. One of the things you do out there with a rod in your hand is confront yourself, and if that confrontation isn't a big, cosmic deal, so much the better.

I WAS getting ready to leave for a fishing trip recently—packing in the afternoon to leave that evening—when Larry called to see if I wanted to go with him and Steve Peterson to fish a certain private bass pond, one I'd heard about and had wanted to get on for some time. He wanted to leave in twenty minutes.

Larry is an expert at wangling himself (and friends, if they're lucky) into secret, private fishing spots, but he's not one to give you a lot of notice. To fish with Larry, you have to be in a more or less constant state of alert. It also helps if you don't have a regular job.

Larry is this way because *he* doesn't have a regular job. When asked what he does for a living, he'll usually be vague. When someone asks me, I say he's a blacksmith who makes beautiful Damascus steel knives, and I may add that he sort of buys, sells, trades, fixes and/or redesigns things. No, I can't be more specific. Things. Anything. Another way to put it is that he's self-employed. In any event, when he feels like going fishing, he usually just goes and the first you hear of it is when he's standing on your front porch in his waders. Sometimes he'll stop to make a quick phone call.

I explained that I was supposed to meet Ed in Palmer Lake that evening for a quick getaway the next morning and was going to try and get a little work done in the meantime.

"So," Larry said, ignoring the mention of work, "we'll go a little early and you can drive your own car. You can leave for Palmer Lake from the pond. The most you'll be is a little late."

Sure, of course, makes sense.

Then I felt this cold nose on my elbow. "Ah, but I'm dog-sitting and the dog's owner won't be out to pick her up until later this afternoon."

"So," Larry said, "leave the door unlocked for your friend. That's a coal black, ninety-pound German shepherd. No one is going to break in."

If this was one of those Walt Disney morality play cartoons, I'd be Goofy and Larry would be the little guy with horns and a pitchfork whispering in my ear, "Forget about what you're supposed to be doing. Go fishing."

I went. I was packed anyway except for a few odds and ends and, after all, this was a *new pond*. I'm not out to hit every good fishing spot in the United States, but I do plan to make a dent—and the bigger the dent, the better.

THE pond was a little over an hour's drive east of Interstate 25, the line that, in my personal cartographic system, officially separates the foothills of the Rockies from the Great Plains. More than that I cannot say. Larry led the way in his silver Cadillac while Steve and I followed in my pickup, with the canoe strapped on top. Larry drove slowly (for him) so that, with the pedal right to the floor, I was able to keep up. Steve and I had only the vaguest idea where we were going.

We pulled off the highway at one of those little towns that

isn't really a town anymore, even though its dot and name are
still on the map. Millie's Cafe, the Feed and Hardware and
the few other once-friendly mom-and-pop operations on
what was formerly a cottonwood-shaded main street were
vacant and filled with nesting sparrows. One or two of the
houses looked like they might still be lived in. What's there
now by way of a business district is a joint baking in the sun
out by the highway, selling gas, beer, pop, junk food and
maps: the bare essentials needed to keep strangers moving
through.

I do patronize these places—one occasionally needs a mi-
crowaved hot dog or a Coke for sustenance—but I hate to see
a place go to seed when what it gets replaced with is of lesser
quality by far. Millie's may once have served the cosmic
chicken-fried steak, but now I'll never know.

To be fair, the new joint serves a predictable hot dog and
the pop *is* cold as advertised. The kid behind the counter
seems a little stoned. Maybe he is, or maybe he's just feeling
the normal effects of working a boring job for minimum
wage.

I guess I'd been in one of those moods lately: you know,
the kind where you don't feel very pleased about things, but
can't quite put your finger on why, although deep down you
know it's just the residual existential nervousness that comes
from trying to make a living and reading too many newspapers.

When I'm at home, my morning ritual involves heading
down to Andrea's Cafe, where I swill coffee and devour a
newspaper pretty much cover to cover, skipping the business
and sports sections. I see this as a kind of civic duty—trying
to keep up, trying not to be ignorant—but so many things are
always going wrong, and they're such big things.

This kind of brooding may not be entirely good for me. I
once overheard a waitress down there saying, "When John
comes in in the morning, I put a cup of coffee on the corner
of the table and push it over to him with a broomstick."

I'd recently told a friend that I'd resolved to only get

pissed off at those things about which I could conceivably do
something. "Good idea," he said, and it was, but I hadn't
actually managed it yet.

On the other hand, when you're on your way to a new,
possibly great pond, these little moments of nostalgia and
self-doubt are short-lived. When you're fishing, you just
want to find this particular pond and then catch that specific
bass. For a time you stop worrying about what you'll want
next.

We got our cold Cokes, and Larry's Cadillac spewed
gravel as he left the parking lot. Driving only 10 or 15 miles
per hour over the speed limit had made him a little twitchy.
To stay in the spirit of things—and to illustrate that my old
pickup isn't exactly a dog—I spewed a little gravel myself
following him. If there had been anyone left in town, they
would probably have disapproved.

It took a while to locate the place and a while longer to get
on the pond. There was the man and his wife to meet, a neat
country spread to be admired, dogs to pet (one with a sore
ear), weather to be discussed: the usual obligatory pleasant-
ries you engage in while trying not to seem too anxious. The
owner would like to have shown us his pond personally, but
he couldn't. Too busy, he said. I told him I knew what he
meant.

The pond, when we finally got on it, was beautiful. It was
big and rambling, amoeboid shaped, lying in a natural swale
out of sight of the road, with old cottonwoods along the north
bank and a cattail marsh lining an arm pointing southwest.
The water was matted with duckweed and there was
bleached, flooded timber for the bass to hide in. Two boats
were pulled up on shore: a canoe in good repair and an
apparently well-used duck boat. The owner was a hunter (his
house was filled with the mounted heads of animals, but no
fish), so I guessed there were more ducks shot here than
there were bass caught. A promising speculation.

A flock of a dozen white pelicans flushed when we drove up, and they wheeled overhead a few times before heading north where, presumably, there was another pond. The herons and coots stayed put, however, apparently willing to share the water with us as long as we behaved. We got into belly boats, struggled out through the weeds and began to fish.

And we caught some: a number of decent bass (one of Steve's was the best at, let's say, 4 pounds) as well as some very respectable bluegills. There are bigger bass in there, according to Larry, who knows the pond and who is seldom wrong about these things, but you hardly ever catch the biggest ones on the first trip, and on those rare occasions when you do, it doesn't seem quite fair.

Then too, we had arrived in midafternoon and we all knew that, regardless of how hard we fished, the hot two hours would be either side of dusk. I'm surprised we caught as many fish as we did.

I knew I wouldn't stay for the main event because that would mean I'd pull in at Ed and Monica's house at three in the morning. We planned to leave for the lake at five, and the fact that I hadn't had any sleep wouldn't mitigate that. So I was sight-seeing and fishing out of curiosity—taking it easy. That night I told Ed that I had stopped to "look at" a new pond, and he knew what I meant.

So we fished the pond for a couple of hours and, although it was a new one to me, I found it completely recognizable. Sure, every bass pond has its own little quirks, and if it's a good one these are worth learning, but on another level this was just "warm water." The fish were where they should have been for the most part, and they bit the flies that should have worked.

I don't mean I wasn't enjoying it. In fact, this feeling of recognition made me enjoy it more than usual. Sometimes fishing is nothing more than the process of airing out the modest skills you've developed over the years, not so much to catch fish as to just go through the familiar, comforting motions. I knew I was fishing at the wrong time of day and, after struggling through the duckweed in the belly boat for a while, I knew I should have used the canoe instead. But this was one of those days when the pressure was off; when knowing what you're doing wrong is almost as good as doing it right.

Steve and Larry stayed until past dark (and did well, I heard later), but I had this appointment with Ed, who'd be wondering where I was. I was also a couple of strange dirt roads from the highway. I figured I'd recognize my way back in daylight, but probably not in the dark.

As I walked back to the pickup from the far end of the pond, it occurred to me that the truck looked pretty good parked out there in the short grass and the slanting, yellow light, its camper shell full of gear, the canoe on top, the bug-spattered windshield. I also noticed it was beginning to take on that squashed, rounded look pickups get with age and use, as if, left to their own devices, they'd eventually evolve into De Sotos.

Maybe it was the idea of having just fished and wanting to leave early so I could fish some more someplace else, but I thought, If I passed this truck on the road, I'd wave.

It also occurred to me, for some reason, that I now had just about everything I'd wanted when I was fourteen years old and was just starting to hang out with the men I admired and wanted to be like. I was all grown up, even to the point of having some gray hair in the beard. I had moved West, where I had a little place outside of town close to a decent trout stream. I had become a pretty good fisherman—maybe not an expert, but one who had seen enough bass ponds that a strange new one had a comfortable, homey feel to it. And I lived in a world that, although far from perfect, was still filled with new secret fishing spots just waiting to be discovered.

I even had a girlfriend with a great figure—something else

I aspired to at the tender age of fourteen, if memory serves me.

(You're right, I should also mention that she's witty, intelligent, an accomplished reporter, reviewer and the business editor of a newspaper, but what we're doing here is looking back into the mind of a fairly typical fourteen-year-old boy in 1959. Okay?)

The fact that all this didn't make me as giddy as I thought it would then was also okay. You're bound to register a little damage over time, losing some of your innocence in the process, but with luck you replace it with what, at certain moments, feels a little like the beginnings of wisdom.

I remember that, as a boy, the men seemed glad and competent in the field, but there was also sometimes a kind of subdued melancholy about them, too. I didn't understand that as a kid, but I do now. Some of those grown-ups gave me what I thought was a hard time then, but by the time I was thirty I'd forgiven most of them, and now, in my forties, I'm beginning to see it's not up to me to forgive anybody for anything. It turned out that life was both more and less serious than they told me it was, but they were just figuring that out for themselves, and how do you get that across to a teenager who just wants to chase girls and catch fish?

Anyway, somewhere in the past, based on the little I knew for sure, I had fastened on the perfect life as one based on art and sport, plus a few other things like love, friendship, pretty country and good food. Given a loose enough definition of art, that's what I had. I didn't get too tangled up in my childhood, though, because I had places to go, more fish to catch and maybe fifteen minutes of daylight in which to find the highway again. I could only spare a minute or two to realize I was happy.

Before I got behind the wheel, I turned to wave at Steve and Larry, but they were out of sight behind some trees. So I stood on the gas and put up a cloud of dust as I left. I thought it was the kind of signal they'd understand.

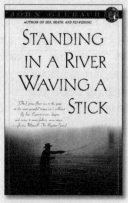

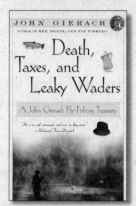